Praise for

C000205002

Mike Kewley writes with the clarity of deep practice about the Perennial Wisdom teachings. His writing is wise yet light-hearted, always drawing the reader back to the magic in ordinary life.

—Piers Moore Ede, author of *Honey and Dust: Travels in Search of Sweetness, All Kinds of Magic: One Man's Search for Meaning Across the Modern World,* and *Kaleidoscope City: A Year in Varanasi*

The true power of Mike's book is its ability to simply and elegantly demystify spirituality and get to the heart of the matter as to why many of us seek. It is an important and much needed work. One that I'm sure will leave a lasting impression on the reader.

—Zahir Khan, Spiritual Teacher and author of *Falling into the Mystery*

The Treasure House

DISCOVERING ENLIGHTENMENT
EXACTLY WHERE YOU ARE

Mike Kewley

It's right in your face,
This moment,
The whole thing is handed to you.

—Zen Master Yuan-Wu

NEW SARUM PRESS
UNITED KINGDOM

Publisher's Note

This publication is designed to provide accurate and authoritative information in regard to the subject matter covered. It is sold with the understanding that the publisher is not engaged in rendering psychological, financial, legal, or other professional services. If expert assistance or counseling is needed, the services of a competent professional should be sought.

Contents

The Myth of Enlightenment

I climbed out of the taxi and stepped into the fierce heat of the Mumbai sun. I had arrived on a quiet sub-urban street in an affluent part of the city, a world away from the colourful chaos of Colaba and the flea-ridden hostel I was staying in for the next month. I glanced at the scrap of *The Hindu Times* on which a friendly German backpacker had hurriedly scrawled an address and stared at the bright new apartment block in front of me. I had finally arrived. This was the home of the most famous guru in the world.

Struggling with my heavy backpack, I made it up several flights of stairs to his room, my clothes already soaked in sweat and my heart hammering in anticipa-tion of our meeting. He would be the first Enlightened Being I had ever met. My spirits sank a little as I arrived at his door and stumbled over a sprawl of shoes, sandals and flip-flops from the other truth seekers who had arrived earlier than me. I had hoped for a private meeting.

I dropped my backpack and tried to make myself look presentable when the door suddenly opened and a bespectacled Indian greeted me with a smile, raising his finger to his lips and gesturing that I should be quiet. He led me through a crowded room to an empty chair in the corner.

I took a few moments to orientate myself. I was surrounded by spiritual seekers from all over the world huddled together on the floor, or sitting in rows of mismatched chairs. Some had their eyes closed, their faces blissful and serene as if all their existential angst had melted away. Others stared intensely at the elderly guru who was speaking passionately about ego, illusion and consciousness.

He wore a simple white *kurta* and—to my mind at least—appeared to be bathed in an aura of soft white light. My eyes fixed upon him, watching him pause now and again to sip from a huge mug of hot, fragrant chai which stated: 'Best Grandad in the World'.

I planned to attend his morning talks for the next month or so, soaking up his wisdom by some kind of spiritual osmosis and moving ever closer to my lifelong goal of enlightenment. From now on everything would begin to make sense. He would tell me what I needed to do, and I would do it. His every word would be divine truth and my liberation was guaranteed.

At the end of the meeting, the guru put his mug of chai down and looked around the room, slowly and deliberately meeting everyone's gaze. A surge of antic-ipation filled the room and we all felt that something profound was about to happen. He then broke into a huge toothless grin and said, "You know, the chance of anyone in this room becoming enlightened, is… ZERO!"

There was a jolt of shock and confusion and then the entire room exploded into ecstatic laughter, so loud that it must have been heard beyond the quiet, affluent streets below. I also found myself laughing wildly as my precious goal of a future enlightenment fell away and a brand-new freedom dawned for the very first time.

Beginnings: the Garden of Eden

I was 29 years old, it was a hot July afternoon and my life, as I knew it, suddenly ended. I was studying in the university library when I happened to notice a book on the shelf next to me by a well-known spiritual teacher. As is often the case in these tales of serendipity the book was in the wrong place, squeezed into the local history section. Feeling as if the book was announcing itself to me, I picked it up, pushed my dissertation to one side, and began to read. Only a few months earlier, in the midst of a deep personal crisis, I had abandoned my 10-year search for enlightenment and I knew that this was probably the last spiritual book I would ever hold in my hands.

But after three or four pages I came across a sentence that made the entire universe stop. I realised that I was unified with the room and everyone in it. In fact, I *was* the room. My sense of being a separate person collapsed and what remained was the direct experience of being nothing and everything.

A surge of terror shot upwards from my belly with such an intensity that I thought I was having a panic attack, but as it rushed into my heart its overwhelming force dissolved gently across my chest, like a firework fading into the night sky.

That was it. My search was over. I finally understood that the elusive and mystical reality I had been looking for had always been on show as everything. I began to laugh out loud as I realised I had spent my lifetime completely overlooking something so simple, ordinary and obvious.

I walked out of the library, sat on a bench in the middle of a small garden and stared at God for an hour. I had never understood that word before, but it now seemed appropriate for the all-embracing reality which had revealed itself. The sparrows hopping in the grass, the flowers and flies, trees and people all shone with a fierce radiance to which I had somehow been blind. I had heard of the burning bush, but this was the burning world.

The veil of duality had disappeared and I understood that I was *home*. In fact, I had always been home, resting in my true nature, sitting in the timeless, non-dual *now*. My mind had been searching for something that was always here. It was all so simple: Mike had never really existed. He had never really been in the way. There was only God—knowing itself, being itself, acting through itself.

This realisation was all the more amazing because it did not take place on my meditation cushion or at the feet of an enlightened guru. I had been practising mindfulness, meditation, self-inquiry and yoga for years in the hope that witnessing my body and mind would somehow bring about the shift into Oneness I desired.

From a young age I had believed that the purpose of my life was to attain Enlightenment and I had searched for it with fervour. I had studied eastern and western philosophy, meditated in silence on long retreats and travelled through India and Pakistan, Nepal and Myanmar seeking the answers that my own culture seemed to have lost. I sat at the feet of famous gurus and spiritual teachers, prayed to Allah for salvation, had peak experiences in the streets of Paris, washed away my sins in the River Ganges and practised *Zikr* with Sufis on a remote Welsh hillside. And yet none of this prepared me for the sheer simplicity of self-realisation.

As I sat on that bench with the sun on my face, my mind was extinguished, I knew that the great mystery of life and death had finally been resolved. We are nothing. We are everything. There is nothing to seek or find.

Finally, I stood up and caught the bus home. By the time I had sat down with a cup of tea the intensity of the oneness which had soaked me to my bones had begun to fade and it seemed as though everything had returned to normal. Apart from one thing: Mike was gone, he had vanished.

Over ten years have passed since that sunny day and although so much has happened, it's equally true to say that nothing has happened. I am not a spiritual teacher or guru, I don't have a lineage or tradition to boast of. I don't wear a costume or use a Sanskrit name.

I had once imagined how extraordinary it would be to live in an enlightened state and had envisaged wandering from place to place, sleeping on park benches and meditating alone in leafy glens, but almost the opposite has happened. After my awakening I returned to the place of my birth, the Isle of Man, fell in love, married and had children. I now teach mindfulness to people interested in training their minds and discovering who and what they are—beyond the narratives they have adopted, the identities they have taken on, or what they have been told by others.

The mystical adventures which defined my 20's stopped and everything became ordinary. Gloriously ordinary. Wonderfully ordinary. It's this ordinary enlightenment that I explore in the following pages. This is the understanding that the freedom and joy we are searching for do not live in a distant temple, ashram, or state of mind, but is our constant and obvious experience. The paths which take us away from our present-moment experience towards a future happiness and wholeness, are merely more distractions.

The path to enlightenment leads nowhere. It's a journey back into the silent depths of who we fundamentally are, not a step away. Wisdom traditions agree that if you want to wake up, above all things, be present.

And yet being present to life's pervasive ordinariness is challenging. It is a tragic irony that our very existence seems necessarily to include the forgetting of just how miraculous it is to exist at all. We are all born into this wonderland called life and yet our day-to-day survival requires that we quickly become over-familiar with it—complacent even—normalising the miracle and then seeking something else on top of it.

In Greek mythology we find the story of Hypnos, the god of sleep, whose cave was surrounded by the river of Lethe. By drinking the waters of Lethe we fall into a deep sleep of forgetfulness, becoming confused about who we really are and what the world really is. To uncover the bright boundless reality which lies at our hearts, we must learn how to awaken from our groggy sleep.

In the following chapters I'll share with you how we can all learn and remember that our own ordinary lives, the lives we try to avoid, suppress and fix, are themselves the living treasures we seek.

We will wander through the ever-changing landscape of each moment and discover how to fall in love with the ordinariness we find there, an ordinariness which is always none other than the divine mystery dancing in front of us, oozing its sensory glory.

Until we recognise this abundance, within and without, we live like birds on the wing searching for the sky or fish seeking the very water in which they swim.

Reality is like an infinite diamond with an eternal number of sparkling facets. To glimpse even one facet with clear eyes can crack us wide open and dissolve the illusion of time, self and other. But if we can learn to keep our eyes open, then we see the miracle, right here and now, as everything and everyone, no exceptions.

It's time for us all to wake up—and remember.

Nothing is Hidden

I grew up on the Isle of Man, a small island rich with leafy glens and sandy beaches in the middle of the Irish Sea. It's a place steeped in Celtic myths and legends but perhaps the most famous concerns *Mannanin Mac Lir,* the god of the sea, who would hide the island from invaders with his cloak of thick grey mist.

But even though I spent my childhood on this misty Celtic Island, I was immersed in another exotic culture of snow-capped mountains and hot dusty plains. My father was a lay Buddhist in the Theravada tradition and his Burmese master, Rwetta Dhamma, would often visit us, his orange robes frequently blowing up around his head in the wild Manx wind.

Surrounded by the teachings of the Buddha, I was aware of the concept of impermanence from a very early age. Our family home was even named *Annica,* the Pali word for the underlying transience of all things. This small wooden plaque that hung by our front door acted as a constant reminder that both the house and its inhabitants were already in a state of flux.

For many years I believed that the realisation of impermanence was a special understanding, a life-changing epiphany that could only happen in the depths of meditation, but the truth is that it's something we experience in every moment. It's what every moment is made from.

For example, can you find the moment you woke up this morning? Or the thought you had ten seconds ago? How about the moment you sat down? These experiences certainly happened it's just that none of them contained any permanence. They were here, but now they are gone.

This is because each moment is not a stable independent experience, but an ongoing movement; a process, which in itself is ungraspable. Every single thought, feeling or emotion we have ever had, came and went, appeared and disappeared, revealing its transient, flowing and ungraspable nature.

But it's not just our everyday moments that are inherently fleeting, even our most profound experiences arise and pass, appear and disappear.

A year or so after my awakening I found myself talking to an Israeli meditation teacher about my experience in the garden, describing the most important moment of my life in vivid detail. When I had finished speaking, she simply looked at me and said, "Ok, but now it's gone. Flushed away."

She was right. The most profound experience of my life was gone. It had been flushed away just like every other moment of my life. All that was left was this particular moment. The question was, could I awaken to that? Could I fully inhabit this new moment without yearning for another?

We are all looking for the big experience, something otherworldly, something transcendent and holy and special. An experience or insight to shift us permanently from the mundane to the divine. But the problem is that as long as we yearn for a particular kind of experience—a spiritual experience—we will be disappointed, simply because it is the nature of every experience to pass away. We might be able to recognise that thoughts, sensations and emotions are passing experiences, but so are moments of bliss, cosmic oneness and astral travel.

Every single moment we have so far enjoyed or suffered appeared and disappeared, came and went, peaked and troughed. Every single moment we have yet to encounter—good, bad or ugly—will also come and go regardless of its content.

The freedom we long for is not gained by chasing a special permanent moment, but by understanding the impermanence of *all* moments.

It is vital to appreciate this, because although we may believe that we are on the path to enlightenment, we are often just travelling back the way we came, attempting to recreate or recapture glimpses of transcendence that somehow trickled through our fingers.

Of course, we feel confused, disheartened or lost when this happens but it's crucial not to take it personally, as if we did something wrong or were not worthy of this fleeting encounter with God. We just didn't understand the impermanent nature of experience because we've never really stopped long enough to stare it in the eye.

Fortunately, this very moment reveals everything we need to understand about the nature of all moments, profane or profound. We don't need to run to the bookshelves and pore over philosophies and esoteric teachings about the nature of reality, when reality is happening right now, as our own intimate and obvious experience.

Even though all our previous moments have been flushed away, the truth is that we have never really lost anything. It is the constant flushing itself that transforms and liberates our relationship with the world. It's how we realise that we're all living in the house of *Annica*.

Our journey is not to arrive somewhere else but to establish ourselves here and now, in this empty moment, this placeless place. By understanding that all potential moments are equally ungraspable, our hunger for a special moment in the future fades away. We will have special moments, epiphanies and realisations, no doubt, but they will pass, this moment will pass, the next moment will pass. It's the transient nature of all things which makes each moment priceless.

For, as a Zen Master of old reminds us[1],

See with your eyes,

Hear with your ears,

Nothing is hidden.

---

1. Cleary, T (trans.) Cleary, J.C. (trans.), Tenkai, 1977. *The Blue Cliff Record*, Shambhala Publications Inc., Boulder, CO.

Each Moment is Yours

When we are feeling broken and desperate, forgotten and alone it is often then that we are closest to a moment of genuine transformation.

This happened for me years ago as a student in Bristol. I found myself sinking into a pit of self-loathing and depression. The meditation practice which had previously given me so much freedom and perspective had fallen away and I found myself overwhelmed by waves of loneliness and alienation.

Feeling mad with despair, I dropped to my knees as tears of heart-wrenching confusion streamed down my face. I hated myself and my meaningless existence and that self-hatred was eating away at me like a black rot that nobody else could see.

Why should I continue my spiritual journey—my journey through life even—If I was not worthy of the enlightenment it promised? I stared out of my window, not knowing what to do next and hoping that some kind of miracle would occur.

It did.

Suddenly a lone seagull soared into view, effort-lessly riding the breeze. I quickly become mesmerised by this gleaming white bird as it hovered, swooped and sailed through the vast blue sky. Then the miracle happened, or rather, I realised that *this moment was the miracle* I'd been hoping for.

I immediately understood that I was the only person alive watching this particular bird, from this particular view, in this particular moment, which had never before occurred in the history of the universe.

This moment was a unique cosmic event and despite my perceived wretchedness, it was freely gifted to me. For the first time in my life, I realised that the extraordinary moment I had been chasing in my meditation practice, was the moment I was already in.

I gazed out of the window for some time like a joyful idiot, the misery and contraction that consumed me only minutes earlier had now dissolved into a deep sense of fulfilment and delicate awe.

I had discovered that each ordinary moment was not something to avoid, battle against or rush through; it was the goal. From now on every dirty dish, fallen leaf or wet bus journey would be soaked in a glory that I had somehow failed to see. For so many years I had tried to emulate the lives of other people— gurus, saints and sages—all the while ignoring the miraculous feat of my own simple existence.

We are all prone to this ignorance, this forgetting. It is part of our journey to authenticity, to being able to stand on our own feet, anchored in this particular life, as this particular person. But until we see this we usually abandon ourselves and go looking for other people's experience of enlightenment, missing the very ordinary miracle of our very next breath, our very next moment.

The truth is that the gifts we seek are all around us. The revelations appear so quickly and so fast that we've forgotten to live in a constant state of awe

Transformation, insight and wisdom are always available, regardless of how we feel about ourselves, but we like to believe that we must first become worthy of the miracle by purging ourselves of all of our human sludge and darkness. We think that we must prove ourselves, put ourselves to the test, achieve something outside of ourselves, and perhaps that does lead to transformation.

But there is another way: we can stop every now and again, whether we are in the stillness of deep meditation or the cold ache of despair, and grace our own little lives with a simple spark of attention.

Use that attention now. Look up and down, left and right, inside and outside. What appears? What is conjured into existence for you? Out of the myriad multiverses what greets you to say hello? A seagull flying through the sky? The bright clink of a teaspoon against a cup? A chair in the corner?

This is the miracle we've been searching for.

You're Lucky to be Alive

There are many profound and earth-shattering insights on the spiritual path, but one of the most valuable is also one of the simplest: the very fact that you exist at all, is a miracle.

During World War Two my Grandfather Jack flew in the RAF as a mid-upper gunner on Lancaster Bombers. Not only did the Lancaster crews have an extremely high mortality rate (a new recruit was expected to survive only two weeks) but his position in a fibreglass turret on top of the plane made him the perfect target for enemy aircraft.

When my brother and I were children he would regale us with stories of his tight-knit international crew (once revealing that his only injury was breaking a tooth on a frozen chocolate bar at 30,000 feet), but there is one particular story that has always stuck with me as if my life depended upon it, because—it did!

They had just completed a mission and were flying home when they happened to notice a lone enemy plane alongside them, tucked away in the clouds and completely unaware of their presence.

It was an easy target and the crew debated whether or not to open fire. Jack, who would have provided most of the firepower, felt that they should stay out of trouble and get home in one piece.

The crew agreed and as their plane veered away they discovered, to their horror, that the single enemy plane they had spotted was actually part of a large squadron. If they had opened fire Jack and his crew would almost certainly all have been killed.

I often reflect that the existence of my mother, myself, my own children (and potential grandchildren) can be traced back to a decision my grandfather made in the clouds, eighty years ago.

Of course, we all have stories like this that reveal the sheer grace of our own existence. But it's remarkable how little attention we pay to the fact that our lives are completely contingent upon an infinite array of other people's past choices, actions and moments.

The fact is that you are only experiencing this moment because every one of your ancestors (who are also my ancestors if we go back far enough) somehow lived long enough to procreate, despite sickness, accidents, wars and ill-fortune. This not only reminds us how ancient our bloodline is but also just how precariously it threads its way from moment to moment, life to life.

Once we start looking we can find this precariousness everywhere. If the conditions for the Big Bang had been slightly different then there might not have been a universe. If the Earth were not in its precise location in our solar system, life as we know it would not exist, and if the meteorite which contributed to the extinction of the dinosaurs had missed the Earth by even a fraction, then there would be no human race to produce your ancestors and bloodline.

Tibetan Buddhists believe that a human birth is a rare event, as likely as a blind turtle swimming in the vast ocean depths, coming up for air after 30,000 years and putting its head through a wooden hoop randomly floating on the surface.

A human birth may indeed be a rare event but your head *is* through the hoop. You *were* born, you *do* exist. And yet there are countless ways in which your journey to the hoop could have been thwarted. You began life as a helpless and dependent collection of fragile cells forming in your mother's womb which have, against all the odds, developed into a unique human life.

To live a life of wonder, awe and gratitude there are two hoops through which we must place our heads. The first is the unlikelihood of human birth, and the second is to *appreciate* the unlikelihood of human birth. Everyone has the first, not everyone has the second. Now that you have this rare and precious birth, this wonderful opportunity, what will you do with it? What *are* you doing with it?

You don't have to cure cancer or reverse global warming. You can begin by understanding that you are a miracle. All your loved ones, friends, enemies and strangers in the streets are walking, talking, laughing, struggling miracles too. One of the most valuable insights you can have is not achieved through years of silent meditation or advanced yogic postures, but through the realisation that you and everyone else, shouldn't really be here at all, and yet—somehow—we have been granted this gleaming sliver of existence.

Close Your Eyes and Count to Ten

Some people come to mindfulness and meditation because they want to have mystical experiences or discover how to awaken from the dream of duality. For others it's much simpler: they just want to have a good night's sleep.

Like so many of us, my 97-year-old grandmother finds it almost impossible to fall asleep each night because of her overactive mind. Scenes from her long life—some joyful, some tragic—play like movies across the screen of her mind, making it difficult for her to relax. Because I have worked with many people who find sleeping difficult, she recently asked me if I could help and so I suggested counting ten focused breaths each night as she lies in bed, rather than swimming in her thoughts.

We've all heard that counting sheep can be an effective way to fall asleep, but counting breaths is perhaps an even older method that takes our focus away from disruptive thoughts, and into the raw sensations of breath passing through the nose. This simple practice also has the benefit of regulating the nervous system and shifting us down a gear, into a state of relaxation, which is ideal if sleep is our goal.

But counting breaths isn't just an effective way to

fall asleep, it is also a powerful meditation technique that allows us to train our attention and manage distractions. We can use this simple technique during the day both to strengthen our concentration power and to shift us into a state of mental, emotional and physical calm.

The practice of breath awareness is often treated as a simple beginner's technique but it has the power to radically enhance our lives. We already know what it feels like to try and focus on the thousands of things that demand our attention throughout the day, but what does it feel like to pay attention to just one thing, deeply and vividly?

We take around 20,000 breaths every day, but how many of those do we saturate in full, unwavering attention?

One reason we find such focused attention so difficult is not that we lack the capacity, but the encouragement. Our 24/7 media culture is defined by distraction, entertainment and a constant stream of information that we have no idea how to manage. Life can *feel* overwhelming because the way we live *is* overwhelming.

Not only does this stream of digital content frazzle our minds, but it also numbs us to our present-moment experience. Recently I was walking along the beach early in the morning as the sun was rising. I noticed a family with their puppy: all the human members of the little group were gazing into their phones, oblivious of the cosmic event unfolding in front of them and ignoring each other. At that moment their puppy was more alive than they were.

These multiple distractions result in a short and shaky attention span, constantly bouncing from one thing to the next like a tennis ball at Wimbledon. This roving attention becomes normal—the way we live—and we soon forget what it was ever like to stop and rest, focused and thought-free in the space of the present-moment.

The good news is that our attention can be trained. By making stopping-points in the day to track 10 focused breaths (and, with practice, 20, then 30, then 40 and so on) we can enter a state of concentration in which our thoughts recede into the background and eventually fade away altogether. The overactive mind which disrupts our sleep, our relationships and our lives, relaxes into a state of tranquility.

This is how we can actively train ourselves to feel happier and calmer, here and now, rather than at some point in the future. The training we do now creates our future relationship to the mind.

We can sometimes become so fascinated by the concepts of enlightenment, awakening and non-duality that it becomes purely an intellectual pursuit. We are far too busy using the mind to remember how to let it go and put it down. Our interest in enlightenment then may even be our downfall if we do not know how to calm our mental traffic.

Counting breaths is not merely a beginner's practice. Each breath is an expression of the universe and all the truths held within it, a merging of emptiness and form, external and internal. The breath is a wise teacher and by concentrating into it we discover that the separation between inside and outside does not exist.

By focusing her attention into her breath my 97-year-old Grandmother is not only learning how to calm her mind and fall asleep more effectively, she is also making herself available to the experience of Oneness, whether she knows it or not.

Regardless of what we do or how we feel, our breath is always available. It is a powerful gateway to extraordinary states of clarity, concentration and calm. The ways in which we live, sleep and relate to the mind and the world are profoundly transformed when we learn how to stop and pay attention to one breath at a time.

And how do we do that? It's easy, just close your eyes and count to ten.

You Contain Multitudes

At the age of twenty-two, I returned home to the Isle of Man after several life-changing months backpacking around Northern India and Nepal. I had embraced a newfound identity during this time and now wore the uniform of Nehru Jacket and *mala* beads which marked me as a Serious Seeker of Truth, walking a path towards inevitable Enlightenment. I meditated, practised yoga, read all the right spiritual books and could hold my own in any tea-house conversation about the meaning of life. I'd even considered adopting a *Sanskrit* or *Pali* pseudonym to make myself appear more mystical.

But something strange was happening: the more I tried to live up to my identity as an advanced spiritual being, the more I seemed to be ensnared by the grit and grime of my ordinary human nature.

I discovered that my new life was not the antidote to my old life that I had imagined, and would find myself battling, ignoring, or even actively repressing, my anger, selfishness and confusion. Instead of neutralising them, my spirituality seemed to give them fresh fuel. I found this contradiction overwhelmingly frustrating. Why couldn't I leap free of my 'lower self'? How could this paradox of light and dark coexist within me? I increased the length of my daily meditations and contemplated how to 'kill' my ego—until I realised that this was just my ego talking.

Then one day I had a flash of insight. I saw that my ego wasn't the problem. It was my attachment to my newfound spiritual identity—the shiny new self I had constructed—which was causing all the trouble. I'd been trying to ignore my human nature by superimposing a new set of ideas and beliefs on top of it and this had the effect of splitting myself in two and instigating a vicious civil war.

Rather than patiently meeting, including and embracing the parts of myself that I deemed unworthy, I had attempted to ignore them to death, plastering over them with exotic ideas and practices. It didn't work: it just made them stronger, as they screamed for the attention I refused to give them.

I had been running towards a goal called 'Enlightenment' in my mind and did not have the time or inclination to wade through the deep egoic sludge of my dark side. Why put myself through all of that when I could simply change my name, wear mala beads and backpack through India?

I've learned that our human nature is not a barrier to freedom and the ego is not an enemy to be exterminated. Our pain, fear and greed are not fundamentally wrong, but fundamentally human. And that is ok because this is the human experience, so let's not pretend it's something else.

Instead of fighting ourselves—our higher nature versus our lower nature—we can go back to basics and return to an experience of who and what we were before we filled our heads with notions of right and wrong, enlightenment and ignorance. We can start again—right now—and meet ourselves in a state of radical simplicity, free from the identities, beliefs and agendas that we have assumed over the years.

We can allow ourselves to rest in that thought-free silent space that allows and unifies all experiences. Like a flower drenched in sunlight, we can unfold from the small contradictory self (which is always a contracted self) into a loving spaciousness in which everything is welcome to emerge and express.

This is perhaps our most human place—a place-less place.

I was surprised that in the months and years which followed, my fascination with spirituality faded and my striving and self-denial reduced dramatically. I was no longer trying to become somebody else or uphold a new identity but began to savour the lush and transient flow of each moment. Each of those moments offered its own form of perfection which transcended my preferences of good and bad.

Walt Whitman, the American poet, expressed the deep peace that comes with deep self-acceptance when he wrote: *Do I contradict myself? Very well then, I contradict myself, I am large, I contain multitudes.*

So the next time you find yourself trapped in a cage of lofty ideals which seem to split you apart from your own ordinary human experience, be patient. Don't fight yourself, don't run. There is another option: stop, breathe and open to the infinite flavours of this remarkable human experience.

Remember, you are large. You contain multitudes.

Wake up and Die

I recently heard someone on the radio say that the Victorians spoke constantly about death, but never mentioned sex, whereas today, we are constantly talking about sex but never mention death. The avoidance of our mortality can find its way into spirituality too and we can often use our meditation practice as a safe hiding place, away from death, decay and suffering.

But the uncomfortable reality is that every time we sit with this mind, breath and body we are edging closer and closer to a long-awaited encounter with the fact of our own mortality. We cannot escape death because we cannot escape ourselves.

To practise meditation is to become familiar with the undeniable fact of death in every moment. Death is not what we think it is, it is not a one-time event waiting for us in the future but our constant companion. There is the death of each thought, sound, emotion, sensation, breath, mood and state of mind. This is a moment of death right now. We die as much as we live, we disappear as much as we spontaneously appear. We are both phoenix and ashes, ashes and phoenix.

But until we notice the intimacy of death we live, ironically, as though we were already dead. By ignoring death, we imagine that we have all the time in the world, and if we have all the time in the world then there is no urgency to change, serve or awaken. We end up daydreaming our lives away without ever stopping to appreciate that these are *our lives*.

So how do we wake up to the preciousness of our own ordinary lives? How can we appreciate the fact that we don't have time to waste, but that *time has us*, and it is constantly passing?

One of my favourite Zen stories concerns Ikkyu Sojun, an iconoclastic Zen Master known as *Crazy Cloud*, who lived in Japan during the fifteenth century.

> *On New Year's Day as revellers celebrated in the streets, Ikkyu danced towards them waving a bamboo pole with a human skull placed on top. Each time someone criticised him for ruining the celebratory atmosphere Ikkyu simply replied:*
> *"This is the truth."*

We may not talk about death but the simple fact is that I will die and you will die, just as everyone else has died. We are not just living, we are always dying too. Death isn't special, but the fact we try so hard to ignore it is.

Without touching the transience of each fleeting moment, it becomes all too easy to disconnect from reality and stumble through life with our eyes squeezed shut, unaware that any moment could be our last.

Ikkyu was alive. Ikkyu was dead. Ikkyu was awake. Ikkyu saw that people daydreamed their lives away. Parading the skull was not intended to frighten people, but to awaken them to the power and opportunity of their own lives. When we can see for ourselves that not even the next moment is guaranteed, then our lives change automatically.

We find this theme of transformation in Charles Dickens' A Christmas Carol when Scrooge (who is more dead than alive) is confronted by his own grave and has an epiphany in which he realises how precious each life is, and always has been. He then promises to live an altered life and becomes reborn, now bursting with the traits he previously lacked—charity, compassion and kindness.

It is only through a sober encounter with death as the shadow of all things, that we can begin to fully appreciate our own wonderful lives, now framed in their proper context. We then stop wasting our time, energy and attention on the things which no longer serve us. Instead, we can awaken to the fact that every moment is a rare and precious jewel that we have all been taught to ignore.

Yes, we will die, but by gazing at Ikkyu's dancing skull we will not dare fall asleep to life again.

This is the truth.

Every Moment is Best

We often romanticise our search for truth and meaning by imagining that they can only be found in a Himalayan cave or deep in the Amazonian jungle. We feel that we are somehow different, special, and that our journey towards cosmic consciousness shouldn't really involve the monotony of a nine-to-five job, family responsibilities or petty chores. We might even believe that it's this daily drudge that keeps us from realising our true potential.

But the reality is that if you can't find the truth in your kitchen, you're not going to find it anywhere else.

The spiritual life is essentially a simple affair. We develop our capacity to be with every moment as it presents itself, merging into it, rather than reacting to it. Meditation is not just something we do on a cushion with our eyes closed but concerns our active relationship to life itself, to people and places, food, money, sex and responsibility. What is that relationship like? Do some moments count and others don't? Because until everything counts, we are still living from fear and reactivity. A Zen story illustrates this:

Banzan was walking through the marketplace when he overheard a conversation between the butcher and his customer. "Give me the best piece of meat you have," said the customer. "Everything in my shop is the best!" replied the butcher, "You cannot find here any piece of meat that is not the best!"

Upon hearing these words Banzan became enlightened.

Every moment is the best. It's always the best because it's the only moment happening. You cannot find another moment in this moment. If we miss that, then we miss everything.

Through practice, we can transform our relationship with any activity by making it an active meditation. This is how the tedious can become transcendent. By focusing into the task at hand, we can enter the *flow state,* an optimum state of mind coined by positive psychologist, Mihaly Czikszentmihalyi, in which we become so immersed in an activity that there is an accompanying sense of timelessness, effortlessness and selflessness.

I've met many people in my workshops and courses who have entered deep states of flow whilst kayaking through rapids, bungee jumping, running a marathon or practising martial arts. But it's not only these more intense activities that can shift us into a radical state of presence. Recently a friend described an experience of walking in her field at sunrise, picking up horseshit. "There's nothing else happening," she explained, "Just me and the poop."

I'm fascinated by these reports because they show us that whenever we become fully absorbed in an activity—any activity—our messy and complicated lives are suddenly reduced to an expansive moment of sheer simplicity.

But what does picking up horseshit have to do with enlightenment? Everything. Transformation happens when we stop running away from our ordinary lives and merge with them. Running away to temples and ashrams can be helpful, but the real test is always when we return to our families, jobs and responsibilities. Have we realised that they too are an act of meditation?

We may be able to find deep inner peace in the structured silence of a meditation retreat, but can we find it in the maelstrom of parenting, marriage and mundane chores? The daily grind of washing-up, hoovering and sweeping need never been an obstacle to rush through with gritted teeth, but a secret invitation to an expanded way of living. Your house, apartment, garage, shed or couch is holy ground and all tasks are sacred.

Every moment is best.

Reflect upon which jobs you have an aversion to. Which tasks trigger resistance or apathy? Which activities do you hurry through absentmindedly because you believe that they are simply not worthy of your time and energy?

Once you have found this tension you can consciously work with it. The resistance comes from imagining that there is another moment to get to, and that mopping the floor is an obstacle. But it's not. It's the best. Each moment is always the best.

Instead of indulging the thoughts and judgements about mopping the floor, try to purposefully focus into the activity of mopping itself, treating it as an act of meditation. This is no longer a chore, there are no chores, there is only the practice of presence. Can you hoover the house and become the hoovering? Can you wash the dishes and realise that you are washing your own mind?

We often fail to see that our spiritual practice is not special at all, it's just life. Cleaning the bin or changing a nappy may not be obvious opportunities for awakening, yet when done with full commitment and focus, they hold the same value—perhaps more.

But it's not just the spiritual life that we romanticise, it's our teachers too. We like to imagine these Enlightened Masters as extraordinary figures, exotic and otherworldly, bathed in an aura of light with flowing robes, soft voices and a holy twinkle in their eye, rather than as factory workers or taxi drivers.

But if we keep our eyes open we can find our teachers in the most unlikely of places, often hidden in plain sight. A friend of mine works for the local council as a street cleaner and just this morning I stopped to talk with him. He told me that he'd been watching a heron standing motionless in the harbour and had become deeply absorbed in its beauty.

"It's all so simple," he said as crowds of office workers jostled past, their eyes screened and their ears plugged, "There's *nothing* we need to do. This is the heavenly moment."

We don't need to travel the world to somehow become one with the universe, we can start by being one with this moment, this ordinary moment, this sacred moment.

Now, go and clean the toilet.

You Have No Choice

One of the main reasons I was drawn to meditation as a teenager was the deep sense of meaninglessness that I felt all around me. The world appeared to be filled with pointless and trivial things which only seemed to feed a culture of superficiality. Like many young people, I felt alienated and wished for another life, a fantasy life set in medieval Japan or ancient India, which I romanticised as being more embedded in reality than my own shiny pop culture.

Like so many of us who feel adrift in a pointless world, I just wanted to feel safe in the midst of my own mounting insecurities. And now that I have spent time teaching and training people who look to self-help, meditation or spirituality for a meaningful way forward in life, I can report that actually, we are not all yearning for cosmic truth. Most of us just want to feel in control.

We mistakenly believe that to feel safe and happy we must first learn to control our thoughts, feelings and emotions. But the problem here is that because we are constantly reacting to everyone around us, we would need to control them too.

But then to be in control of everyone else, we would have to influence their thoughts, emotions, and actions, which would mean controlling their interests, personalities, conditioning, parenting and genetics. To achieve that, we would need to control entire cultures, their environment and ultimately the planet itself. But even the Earth is influenced by interplanetary forces, the sun and moon, solar storms and meteorites...

It took me years of desperate searching to understand that to really be in control of my life I would need to be in control of the whole universe because the two are not separate.

The truth is that we have never been the managing directors of our lives. We are not really in control. The idea that everyone is walking around actively choosing which thoughts to think and feelings to feel is nothing but an entrenched myth.

Do you know for certain what your very next thought will be? Or what the next 10 seconds will bring? Can you even be sure that this is not your final breath? We don't know because we have never known. We have lived our entire lives up to this moment in a constant state of unknowing. The mind does its very best to predict and simulate the future for us, but as far as the raw actuality of each moment is concerned, these are just comfort blankets in the wilderness.

And yet something remarkable is happening. Despite never actually knowing what the very next moment would contain, we are still here. We have survived. How is that possible? It's possible because we don't need the mind to micromanage every single moment of our lives. Helpful as it is for some practical matters, the mind knows nothing beyond this moment, it can only tell us a story. Only one thing is certain: you cannot help but respond in some way to whatever happens, just as you have responded in some other way to whatever has 'happened next' on past occasions.

The revelation that I was not the managing director of my life was spelt out to me by an Indian guru. Every day he would ask me to choose an action that I felt completely responsible for, like ordering a cup of chai or crossing the busy street at a certain time. He would then meticulously deconstruct my apparent ownership of this choice by highlighting all the previous causes and conditions, internal and external, cultural and physical, universal and personal, which had led inexorably to that precise moment and exact choice.

At the end of our meetings, I always learnt that— no matter what it was—I had never actually chosen anything. *Life* had. My free will wasn't really mine, it belonged to a much greater movement. From then onwards I felt as though the universe was present in my every thought, feeling and action. Rather than feeling robbed of my freedom, I felt joyously free.

We are never the controllers we imagine ourselves to be. It has taken billions of years for this body to be born, for this moment to arise, for this decision to be made. We may feel like independent entities but the truth is that we cannot even scratch our nose without the support of the cosmos.

Much of our seeking for enlightenment is really the search for more control, more power, more knowledge. But the real freedom lies in our ability to let go and trust in our capacity to respond intelligently to whatever happens next. You can do it because it's all you've ever done.

What choice do you have?

Walk Softly and Be Amazed

How can we see, feel or hear anything with clarity when we live our lives in habitual fast-forward? In the chaos of our day-to-day existence speed is often of the essence (or so we are led to believe) and so we cannot always afford the luxury of consciously slowing our pace, or packing the shopping bags in glorious hyper-real slow motion. We may pride ourselves on being able to whizz through the day ticking off the tasks as we go, but the downside is that the crispness of life is smudged into a meaningless blur.

The simple act of walking mindfully—slowly and attentively—is a powerful way to reclaim some of the intensity and vividness that we seem to have lost. When I first encountered the practice of walking meditation I dismissed it as less important than my formal sitting practice, because I assumed that I already knew how to walk, how to put one foot in front of the other, how to move from A to B, but as it turned out, I didn't.

Now I always include periods of walking meditation on retreats as a way to integrate attention and movement, presence and action. During these sessions I suddenly ring a bell as a signal for everyone to freeze on the spot, our muscles tensing as we try to hold our bodies—and minds—absolutely still.

When the chime fades we continue to walk again or rather *be walked*, our feet automatically stepping in front of us, somehow perfectly managing our balance and weight without any extra involvement from us.

Gently, the mind falls silent and softly unifies with the shifting texture of each new step. Walking begins to happen by itself without any thought of arriving somewhere special. Each footstep becomes a profound communion with the very ground it arises from and, ultimately, returns into.

By immersing our movements in deep attention like this we can also be struck by the incredible efficiency of this body we inhabit (yet did not ask for) as well as its continuous vulnerability. This body is given to us freely and yet its fragility is unavoidable. What a miracle it is then to be able to take even one fervent step forward! How humbling to fully experience each step and yet observe how it fades and vanishes before our eyes.

Such a conscious slowing down allows a simultaneous opening up as our sphere of awareness expands to include all the riches of the world that our fast-paced lives were unable to see. On retreats, we will often walk outside in the garden or amongst the trees, sometimes with the sun warming our faces, at other times with the delicate sting of the rain. It is here, when we are present and still in the midst of nature, that we can have a long sought-after encounter with the real world which springs forth to greet us like a long-lost friend.

A kestrel hovers silently above us, a raindrop resting on a bamboo leaf effortlessly reflects the entire landscape, and the heavy gush of a river in spate becomes inseparable from ourselves.

This is the beauty, wonder and interdependence with which we reconnect each time we slow down and resist the mind's urge to skip ahead. The richness and splendour of the real world is always here and always available, it's just now that we can see it for ourselves. In fact, it's only now that we are *really seeing, really hearing, really feeling.*

Everything else was just noise.

To access the real world (which we were always told was somewhere else) all we have to do is walk without the thought of arriving and be fiercely present to each step, a step which merges into the ground and a ground which is none other than the world.

It's then that we find ourselves inhabiting a magical new reality that both enchants and supports us at every step of our own unique journey to nowhere, cradled in a boundless and unflinching love that has always held us in its intimate embrace.

Here Be Dragons

Just as explorers sailing into new territory may have believed that they might sail off the edge of the world, we too may feel anxious and apprehensive when we consider what the spiritual path has in store for us. We may be longing to awaken like our heroes, but what will it really be like to live without a sense of self, separation and control? When we contemplate the reality of awakening it may become a source of terror rather than comfort.

These are the natural concerns of a mind anxious about falling off the edge of its world, into the vast depths of the unknown. Awakening is where the dragons and sea monsters live, ready to devour us. No wonder the mind wants us to drop anchor permanently in the shallow seas of the known. But if we do not venture forth into the new, unknowable territory we will never transcend its parameters and find out who we are beyond its stories.

As someone who yearned for enlightenment since the age of 7 or 8, I have had many encounters with the dragons of the unknown, moments where the solid ground of the known has suddenly given way to the sheer terror of what Rudolf Otto, the German theologian, called the *Mysterium Tremendum et*

Fascinans, the great and terrible mystery.

Many years ago I was lying in bed and meditating as I fell asleep. I suddenly realised with a shock that I was not the voice in my head, I was the one listening to it and that the listening was a black void which was incomprehensibly vast. My body immediately became paralysed with intense fear and no sounds came out when I tried to scream for help. The back of my head appeared to fall away, like a trap door, and beneath me lay a fathomless emptiness. That emptiness was death. The death of everything I had identified myself as. The death of the mind. In my terror, I clung on and resisted falling with every fibre of my begin. The experience faded and I found myself able to move again. I lay in my bed fully awake and completely ter-rified. What had just happened? I switched on my lamp and slowly surveyed the room. Something was different. The room looked strange. And then it hit me, I was no longer *in* my bedroom—my bedroom was in *me*.

A terrifying shift had occurred and the external world I knew so well was now taking place entirely within my mind. This was not the smooth initiation into Oneness I had anticipated but disorientating and destabilising. In my desire for enlightenment had I tumbled into madness? The experience lasted 3 or 4 days until it began to fade and the world thankfully resumed its external location.

This experience made me question whether enlightenment was something I really wanted. Could I cope with another fall off the edge of the world? And yet, I knew that it couldn't be any other way. This is what I had signed up for when I began my formal meditation practice as a teenager. I was determined to walk the path which led towards illumination, not mere comfort.

On this journey, we will encounter equal moments of gut-wrenching terror and sublime beauty. The scales will fall away from our encrusted eyes and we will be confronted by life as it really is without names or labels, and it is overwhelming. We have heard stories about dragons, but now we are actually wrestling with one, and it wants to bite off our head.

We often believe that we must spend years—even lifetimes—walking the spiritual path before getting lucky enough to catch a glimpse of the divine, but the opposite is also true—the divine is also looking for us. Whether we are meditating in silence or dropping the kids off at school, the Great and Terrible Mystery is always waiting to strike. Over the years of teaching mindfulness to people, I've had the privilege of being witness to transformational moments where the small egoic mind is suddenly confronted with a brand-new world.

During a walking meditation, a woman looks down at the 100-year-old floorboards beneath her and in a flash becomes aware of every foot that has ever stood on it, the carpenters who cut, sawed and shaped it, the tree from which it came and the woodland where it stood. A young man recognises that if he is aware of his thoughts, then he cannot *be* his thoughts, and laughs as he realises that he does not know who he is. An elderly lady follows her breath all the way down into the pause at the end of her exhalation and discovers a vast oceanic space, too big and boundless for her to comprehend. On a silent retreat, a man is suddenly hit with the realisation that he is *dust* and, through his tears, he experiences waves of gratitude and love.

These are just a few descriptions of how the mystery can make itself known to us, revealing a brand-new reality about which we know absolutely nothing. But for some of us, this sublime and enchanted world was never hidden to begin with. As a young boy, the Indian mystic, Ramakrishna, fainted in ecstasy on seeing a flock of cranes soaring across a dark blue cloud. We, however, do not faint at clouds, become overwhelmed by floorboards or become startled at the depths of our own boundlessness. We do not see God in the clothes peg, the sunset, or the stranger in the street. We are blind to the living world and deaf to its music simply because we already believe we *know* what it is and *who* we are.

But the reality is that we don't. We have no idea

what the world really is or who we really are. You didn't choose your name, it was given to you by your parents. It's just a label, a sound, which had been added to your own mysterious being. That beingness has no name and cannot be limited or defined by any label or concept.

It's the same with the world. To discover what it really is we must forget all about it. Even to call it a *world* is just a name. We must unburden this reality from its names and stories and see it afresh as vibrant, amorphous being. We must see with our eyes and not our minds. We must live in the deep astonishment that there is anything to see at all. Then we are sailing in the right direction, into a new nameless reality, falling gladly over the edge of the known.

It's Always Now

When we sit down to meditate, what exactly are we doing? Where are we trying to get to? What is our destination? The word *practise* suggests that we are using effort to produce or achieve something which is not already happening. Many of you will say: "We want to be present in our lives; we want to live in the present moment." This is a noble endeavour, but have any of us ever really been absent in the first place?

But what if presence wasn't something to practise but something to realise? Have you noticed that everything around you right now is resting in a deep state of meditation? For the walls, tables and chairs, there is no past leading to a present, no present leading to a future, but only the *eternal now*. We don't need to teach a crow, a tree or a mountain to meditate because they already exist in an effortless state of unbroken being. What we need to do is become quiet enough to absorb their transmission of eternity.

This is what Vincent Van Gogh was communicating to us through his vivid, hyperreal paintings of sunflowers, stars and cypress trees. He was transmitting their holy timelessness, so that we could see—really *see*—without the mundane overlay that clouds our usual perceptions. When we stand in front of one of Vincent's paintings, gaze at a snow-capped mountain or watch a murmuration of starlings swirl across the sky, we too step out of time and into eternity. *What I know of the divine sciences and the Holy Scriptures, I have learned in woods and fields. I have no other masters than the beeches and the oaks,* said Saint Bernard of Clairvaux. Nature is eternal and invites us to remember our kinship with it.

Like the trees and fields, we are also an expression of nature and yet we ignore this invitation to eternity and seek the timeless while trudging through time. We overlay and divide our experience of the timeless present, into decades, years, months, minutes and seconds, exchanging effortless being for the relentless tick of the clock.

The female mayfly lives for only a few hours, but because she cannot conceptualise herself and fragment her experience of being into past, present and future, she is timeless. We may live to be 100 years old and yet our lives are spent trying to stop, avoid or fill every second, whereas the ephemeral mayfly lives in eternity.

The antidote to striving to be present is to understand that we are *always* present. Like the tree or crow, we also inhabit the timeless now. Does a newborn baby know what time it is? Do your hands or feet know if it is Monday or Tuesday?

We may argue that we are no longer present when

our minds wander into memories or daydreams, but we are still present to the fact of our wandering minds. It is vital to understand this: the content of our minds and bodies does not interfere with the basic fact of our own presence. We are always present to that content. Every moment is a moment of presence. If we were not always present, then we would not even be aware that the distraction was happening. Freedom and insight come not from trying to be present, but from realising that there is a part of us that is never absent.

If we are always present, then there can be no distractions from it. The drowsy mind or nagging thought, the pain in our shoulder or the piercing mechanical rattle of the workman's drill are not obstructions to the present moment, but equal expressions of it.

You can be focused only here and now and you can be distracted only here and now. There is only the here and now however you experience it. Everything happens now. Or, to put it another way: now happens, as everything. So, can we ever leave the present moment? No, the feeling of leaving the present moment is just another present-moment experience.

There is no location called 'past' or 'future'. They are virtual realities that only appear here and now. They have no ground and as such, we cannot build anything there. Confusion and crisis can only exist when we fuel an imaginary past, moving into an imaginary future, to heal or enlighten an imaginary self.

There is only *this* which is always *here* and that *here* is always *now*. It can be neither lost nor gained. There is *only* meditation, arising here and now as everything.

Once we see through the concepts of past, present and future even our most convincing stories can lighten and fade away. For instance, we understand that the universe is 13.8 billion years old and yet it only appears now, in this moment. Where are the vast spans of cosmic time which led to this particular moment? We may be able to imagine them, but we cannot touch them. They are mere concepts. The reality is that the universe is eternal. It is timeless. It only appears now.

It's the same with our personal narratives. At this moment we cannot find or grasp something called *my past* and neither can we find something called *my future*. Yes, we may be able to conjure up memories or imagine tomorrow morning, but all of that also happens right now, in the present moment, the only moment, which contains the notion of all other possible moments.

The mind is a clock. It tells us that we exist in time, that we were born in the past and will die in the future, but our direct experience reveals something radically different—our own timeless being.

The Quiet Enlightenment

The great Japanese *haiku* poets had the great gift of seeing each moment clearly, without the intervention of their thinking minds. Whether they were watching cherry blossoms gently drifting to the ground, or a frog suddenly leaping into a pond, their state of watchful presence allowed them to see things as they really were, conveying it to us in a pithy poem of just seventeen syllables, attempting to capture its bright essence. A *haiku* records a moment of clear seeing rather than a moment of thinking. It's a glimpse of reality, witnessed by nobody.

The practice of mindfulness also allows us to become *haiku* poets of sorts, not just seeing each moment clearly, but being with it in all its unique *suchness*. When we live in our heads we disconnect from our raw and unfolding real-time experience; we live an imaginary life of names, labels and judgements, rather than one blossoming in the present moment.

The rewards of daily mindfulness practice are rich and bountiful but getting up early every morning to sit in meditation and patiently watch the breath passing through our nose, can soon become a chore for the excitable seeking mind which craves action and drama. We sit and sit, and sit, and often nothing of consequence seems to be happening. We may have heard of other people's spectacular experiences of bliss, profound insight or even enlightenment, and yet none of these things ever seem to happen to us. We may spend years, decades even, meditating without really knowing what we are actually looking for.

But even as we sit quietly in meditation, waiting for the thunderbolt of transformation to strike, there is another kind of profound experience happening, a quiet enlightenment which is gently unveiled every time we sit in the depths of our present-moment experience.

When we track the flow of breath through our nostrils the activity of the mind fades into silence like a cloud dissolving back into the vast sky. We are now resting in a state of *samadhi*, a state of no-mind where the separate self, the seeking and the sought all collapse into the silence of our awareness. The momentum of thought, memory, and time is absent while the physical and emotional tension which accompanies them melts away, leaving an all-encompassing sense of easy being.

This simple absence of a separate, seeking self is the very thing we are searching for and yet we imagine it to be achieved *by* the mind, not by the cessation of the mind. When there is no mind to disconnect from the moment, there is no self and where there is no self, there is no seeking, no duality, no story and no problem. We are no longer in the moment—we *are* the moment. This is non-duality.

This is the bliss we have been waiting for. It may seem ordinary and mundane because it does not announce itself with fanfare and yet it is a state free from trouble, disruption and distraction. Now, we are seeing things as they are, hearing things as they are. There is no mind arising to contract our boundless experience into static thoughts and images. We are the *haiku*.

The real value of practice is that it allows us to know ourselves without the veil of the thinking mind. It reveals what we really are, rather than what we think we are. And without the mind to tell us a story, who are we? *What* are we?

This is the enlightenment we are searching for—the quiet enlightenment. It is always present and this is why we miss it. We simply disappear into it each time we meditate. We lose our mind, but we find an ocean of bliss. In this profound reduction of who and what we are, every sound, sight and sensation reveals itself as a unique and fleeting masterpiece of creation, witnessed by no one.

The practice of meditation is not aimed at achieving enlightenment in the future, but suspending the momentum of the seeking mind and searching self, revealing our own inherent bliss here and now. This is how we discover our own sanity, our own inner silent and pristine clarity, which transforms our experience of the world into ecstatic living poetry.

Dig Your Self

I have been digging for treasure all my life. One of my first loves was archaeology and I would spend hours in hedgerows, trowel in hand, digging down through the turf into forgotten farm middens and bringing shards of pottery into the clear light of day.

As I grew older and became more interested in the power of meditation to alleviate my anxiety and depression, I realised that it too involved a form of digging. My trowel was replaced with focused attention and the midden became my own inner strata of thoughts, feelings and emotions.

But I wasn't just digging for inner peace. My real goal was to discover my true Self which I believed lay hidden within me somewhere. I wanted to know who I really was beyond my mind and body and so for years I dug, diligently excavating my own sense of self. In this process, I uncovered some exquisite finds which shone like diamonds but also unearthed cumbersome fossils, the difficult parts of myself which had become frozen in time.

Despite my best efforts, I still couldn't find what I was looking for. There were no cosmic experiences of Enlightenment, no floods of Divine Light, no booming Voice of God to congratulate me. Each time I looked deep within myself all I found was a silent emptiness, a fathomless darkness that lacked any shape or form.

This was disheartening. How could I fail to find my true Self if it was who I really was? How could I look within and find nothing? What was I missing?

But then one day I had a terrifying epiphany. What if my true Self wasn't something, but nothing? What if the mystical realisation I was waiting for, was to simply recognise that, at the very heart of myself, I was nothing at all! I may have failed to find myself as something but this incessant digging had revealed my underlying nothingness.

This dark silent nothingness which lies at the very heart of our being is the very thing we are searching for. It is not an object. It has no colour, shape or size. It is *That* which is aware of all things. The reason we cannot find it, is because we *are* it. We are already seeing, hearing and perceiving *from* this empty silent awareness.

From the very start we are already what we seek. Even if we do have a spiritual experience of love, stillness, peace or oneness, then that is just another experience that takes place within our true Self.

But the mind is like a cloud searching for the sky and yet never really grabbing hold of anything solid or permanent. It looks outwards into the world of experience for its true identity rather than turning inwards to dissolve into its own silent source. It tries to create

DISCOVERING ENLIGHTENMENT EXACTLY WHERE YOU ARE

a stable identity from an ever-shifting stream of perceptions and this is why it is always dissatisfied. There is no solid ground here, only an endless flow of appearances which it tries to snatch and make its own.

Like a lost child desperately searching for its mother, the mind does not realise that it is already cradled in her loving arms. All it needs to do is turn around and look back into her dark, fathomless eyes to realise that the very thing it desires is already here.

To do this all that is required is a simple shift of attention. Like the lost child we can also look back into our own mother, our own true Self. But how do we do that? It's simple: we shift our focus away from the foreground of thoughts and feelings and into the still, ever-present background in which these experiences occur. We turn our attention around 180 degrees and look back into the depths of our own essence. This is the reverse path, the way home.

It's a simple instruction that often creates much confusion because the mind is always looking for an object. Its job is to conceive of who and what we are as a thing, an experience, a person, a separate self and yet when we do turn our attention back on itself, none of these things can be found.

Try it now. Close your eyes and look back into your own essential awareness. Gaze back into your own silent mind.

What did you notice? Common responses include...

I looked back, but there was nothing there.

What was I supposed to find?

It must take a lot of practice because I found nothing at all.

Failure to find anything may be disappointing, but the people who made the statements above are on the brink of a life-changing discovery: there is no solid self, ego, controller, observer or witness to be found.

What there is, *is*. This is the real buried treasure we have been searching for. The surprise is that it is hidden neither in the mountains nor in the deserts. It is not buried deep underground or on a distant planet. It is found in the blind spot, the one place on earth that we would never think to look: *within* ourselves, *as* ourselves.

The true Self is who we are before we start looking for it. The awakened mind is already perceiving these words as you read. The reality of the universe is the reality of you and me. When we search for ourselves externally we find the beautiful and shimmering mirage of the world which is always slipping through our fingers, but when we turn around and look within we uncover the depths of our own dazzling darkness, the true Self which we imagined we had lost.

Keep digging until only space remains.

It's Just This

There is a story I love about the eccentric and often controversial spiritual teacher, George Ivanovitch Gurdjieff. One day, whilst sitting in the Parisian cafe which he used as an office, he was approached by an English aristocrat who offered to pay him £1,000 if he could tell her the meaning of life. Gurdjieff took up her challenge and beckoned a nearby *cocotte* to join him at the table.

He offered her a piece of the cake he was eating and began to tell her an incredible story: he was in fact an alien from another planet and the cake she was eating was a delicacy that had been painstakingly transported to earth from his distant homeland. Nonplussed by his extravagant claim, the streetwise woman took a bite. "It's just almond cake", was her flat reply. Delighted at this, Gurdjieff turned to the aristocrat and triumphantly announced, "That is the meaning of life!" Confused and embarrassed the aristocrat hurried away but legend has it that she later returned to the cafe and paid him his prize money.

The truth is simple, but we don't like simple.

In this story, Gurdjieff cleverly engineers a social role reversal and allows the streetwise *cocotte* to teach the aristocrat that the meaning of life is not a complicated mystery, but completely ordinary. It is the taste of almond cake and nothing more.

The *more* is what we add to it and our mind is an adding machine. If we are looking for inner peace, happiness or freedom, then the mind cannot help. It can only create a problem or solve a problem. It cannot give us peace because the mind itself is turbulence. It cannot show us reality, it can only create a story *about* reality. Its marvellous activity is also its limitation.

It is only when we can relinquish the mind that the sheer simplicity of the moment reveals itself. What remains, is what *is*. Naked reality staring back at us. No self, no separation and no time. There is only the present moment which is both ungraspable and unbounded. There is nothing to gain other than this nakedness, this self-evident reality that cannot be named, defined or labelled.

The mind asks endless questions: *Where is happiness? What is the meaning of life? Who am I?* But our own awareness rests as pristine silence. For the mind which lives in time, happiness must be earned and it imagines that it must first jump through the hoops of religion, philosophy and mysticism in order to find genuine fulfilment or win the prize of Enlightenment. The very notion that everything it seeks exists here and now is completely alien to the mind; the mind is always a movement away from the eternal now.

If I were to ask my 6-year-old daughter about the

meaning of life, she would look bemused. Not because she doesn't know the answer, but because the question itself makes no sense. Life *is* sense. It is none other than our unfolding sensory experience. There is no other life, no other meaning. It's like looking for the sun and ignoring the light which allows us to search. The notion that life has a special or hidden meaning is symptomatic of a mind which has become disconnected from the childlike fulfilment of simply being in the moment.

This is why our greatest teachers are not other human beings with heads full of concepts—however practical—but the natural world, which offers a direct and nonconceptual transmission of reality. This is why Jesus asked us to consider the lilies of the field and the Buddha held aloft a single flower. The Eastern masters encourage us to look at the moon and not stare at the finger that points to it. Gurdjieff offers us a slice of almond cake and in a sense he is not lying to us, the cake really is a rare alien delicacy. Its existence is entirely dependent upon a random collision of other fleeting phenomena, from eggs, flour, and sugar to the existence of the earth and the arising of an individual consciousness to perceive the cake in the first place.

The taste of the cake is the taste of life, rich with cosmic meaning and profound interconnectivity. Every single object is miraculous, it's our over-familiarisation with the world which leads us to forget just how impossible and otherworldly everything really is.

So what is the real meaning of life? As long as you are searching for it, you won't find it.

There is No Escape

The Buddha died from food poisoning, Socrates drank hemlock and Christ was crucified. Al-hallaj was executed, Ramakrishna, Ramana Maharshi, Gurdjieff and Nisargadatta all succumbed to cancer whilst countless wise women were persecuted and burnt at the stake.

Many of us walk the spiritual path believing that we can somehow bypass the human condition and all the blood and guts we find there. Perhaps if we do enough meditation, yoga, breathing techniques or positive thinking we can transform ourselves into superhuman yogis or yoginis free from the ravages of sickness, old age and death?

We practise so that we can become shinier, happier people, rather than use our practice to see that the very nature of the mind is to seek comfort. This usually means ignoring the reality.

The reality is shocking. However special or spiritual we believe ourselves to be, we are just a heartbeat away from death. Remember that the Buddha died from food poisoning. He was an enlightened being and over the course of his lifetime, thousands of people were awakened in his presence and yet in the end he died an ordinary death from something overwhelmingly mundane.

For many years I tried somehow to avoid these difficult truths which were inherent within my own existence and was drawn to anything which promised the good news of love and light. I didn't really want to be here in this body, in this moment, in this particular life. My real goal was not to find truth but to hide from it, and so I travelled to exotic lands and studied mysterious philosophies in order to discover something special, something transcendent, only to come crashing back down to earth afterwards to find myself sitting in the middle of my own rotten life.

I was attempting to live in a state of detachment from myself as an observer or witness of my troublesome thoughts and unwholesome body. This step-back did grant me a new dimension of freedom but I was actively avoiding the juice, texture and flow of my own aliveness. I wasn't just a meditator, I was a ghost—drained of substance.

To inhabit my life fully, I realised that I would have to do something other than simply transcend it. The struggle to remain as the observer of our thoughts is not the ultimate truth, it's a mere tactic, and sooner or later the ability to transcend this moment collapses into the realisation of *immanence*. This is the discovery that there was never a need to escape or avoid this moment because God already dwells within it, *as* it.

This whole universe is Brahman, states the

Chandogya Upanishad, reminding us that it is the presence of the divine within every moment, thought and feeling, which rouses us from the illusion of somehow escaping ourselves through an act of transcendence. The freedom we long for is not to be found in the cold detachment *from* life, but as the sheer and boundless intimacy *with* it.

Each breath is a gateway, each sensation and sound, a portal. We don't need to travel to India to sit at the feet of a guru in *satsang,* when the real *satsang* is each moment.

There is no magic trick to escape the hard yards of old age sickness and death. So much of what passes for spirituality is just another cunning plan hatched by a frantic monkey-mind, looking for a way out. But the real good news is that there is no way out, there is only the way *in,* the way *here,* the way *home.*

Real progress is not measured by how many blissful spiritual experiences we have, but in the difficult, vulnerable and painful moments where we can no longer pretend or hide. The moments when even our most cherished spiritual practices cannot save us. If we can relax into these moments we may discover that they are not the dead-ends we imagine but invitations to find God everywhere as everything.

Split a piece of wood, and I am there, says Jesus in the Gospel of Thomas, teaching us that even when our lives are torn down and broken, shattered and wrenched apart, we never leave the embrace of our divine intimate nature.

Be as Little Children

In the Zen stories I read as a teenager I found it surprising that it was often the poor and illiterate farmers who seemed to realise enlightenment with more ease than the clever scholar monks who became tangled in their own conceptual webs. Such stories tell us that reality is not something we need to understand intellectually, but something we simply need to see. Our mind is a powerful and cunning tool, but it is the softer qualities of innocence, vulnerability and playfulness that finally bring us home to the joy of the mystery.

I've always found that the story of Jesus' nativity points to the power of such simplicity. Christ the Saviour is born not in an opulent palace but in a lowly stable surrounded by animals and simple shepherds. The King of the World has arrived, but he's rather understated. He is neither an emperor nor a politician, he's a helpless newborn baby.

A crying infant may seem to lack the might and power of a world-changer but it's his natural spiritual qualities that mark him out as a special being. Christ the newborn is innocent and pure because he is brand-new to the world. He lives outside of time because the conceptual chains of past, present and future do not yet bind him. He carries no identity, culture or dogma; on the contrary, he is fresh, open and new. He has not yet become dissatisfied with life because he *is* life, shining brightly in the eternal moment.

This fragile baby has no ego, no self and no sense of separation. He does not seek the mystery, he *is* the mystery. He is the King of the World because he *is* the world, it is only those who feel separate from it that need to take it by force.

This is why becoming a parent can be such a transformative experience. Like the infant Christ, our children invite us into their bright new world, free from concepts of time, money and judgement, complications and separate competing selves. Our children cannot enter our world and so we must bow down to theirs, leaving our clever concepts at the nursery door and meeting them in the midst of their own wonderful timelessness. Here we can exchange our overthinking minds for the freedom of sponta-neity and play, spiritual qualities which are so often overlooked or sidelined.

Jesus' nativity expresses clearly that what we ulti-mately seek is to be found in the humblest of places, where the mystery hides as the lowly and apparently worthless. We learn that if we can put our cleverness to one side, just for a moment and rest without the thoughts, names and labels which clutter our minds, we can be infants once again; Kings (or Queens) of

the World held in the manger of the eternal moment,
no longer seeking anything, but finding everything.

The Kingdom of Heaven is yours, if you can see it.

The Joy of Self

Even though my awakening was astonishing in its ordinariness, it had an extraordinary impact upon my mind.

That sentence I had read in the university library was like a nuclear bomb which had detonated in my head, destroying the infrastructure of past and future, self and other, seeking and enlightenment. It had all collapsed. From the gravel on the road to the bubbles swirling in my coffee, everything now had an intense beauty to it which brought me to tears. It was as though my face had fallen away and I was merged with everyone I encountered.

This continued for several months. Outwardly, I was able to function as normal, going to work every day and taking long walks in the forest, but inside, everything had been transformed. Until one morning I woke up to discover that something had shifted: the infrastructure of my mind—that bombed-out city— was becoming energised again and a sense of contraction was emerging to replace the blissful openness I had been floating around in so happily.

I arrived at work in a state of irritation. I had heard stories of people who had experienced awakening only to slip back into a state of seeking months or even years later. Was this now happening to me? I sat at my desk and not knowing what else to do, I closed my eyes and dropped my attention into the mental and emotional activity which has been absent for so long. And then it struck me:

Ah! It's this too!

And suddenly I was laughing again, I was whole again. I had not lost anything. I had only expanded my understanding that this marvellous activity of thoughts and feelings, this activity called *Mike*, had never been in the way. It *was* the way. I had spent so many years trying to deny that I was somebody that I had forgotten the joy of being a *person*.

I felt *Mike* as a welcome energy, a long-lost brother that had suddenly returned to tell me that he too was an expression of the universe.

I feel sorry for the way we treat the separate self in spiritual circles. We are forever trying to kill it, remove it, starve it or repress it as if it were the problem. But actually, we don't need to get rid of this self simply because there isn't one to begin with. There is a *sense* of being a separate self but no *actual* separate self. It is not a problem to be removed but a pattern to be understood.

The separate self is an intelligence. And where did this intelligence come from? Did you choose to experience yourself as a distinct individual, separate from the world around you, or did the experience of separation just happen at some point? Is the ego a mistake the universe has made? Or do we simply view it as a mistake?

Just consider the other intelligent functions occurring right now in your body (which are also patterns the universe has made). As you read these words your stomach is digesting food, your immune system is maintaining your body's health, your heart is pumping blood. Are they mistakes? If we switch off this activity will we become enlightened?

Our sense of being a separate self is not the enemy. It's just activity. It's the expressive and intelligent creativity of the cosmos. There is no-one doing this activity. There is a unique personality in everyone, but you will never find the person.

For years I had believed that the obstacle to enlightenment was myself. Through hours of meditation I had tried to vanquish this foe, and yet he would always return at some point, bubbling with thoughts, ideas, emotions and reactions. I had assumed that the enlightened state was devoid of personality and yet this didn't tally at all with my own experience of the enlightened people I had encountered.

They actually seemed to have *more* personality and energy. These people were not stone buddhas devoid of feeling, but overflowing with wisdom, compassion and humour. Think of your favourite wisdom teachers, are they dull? Insipid? Lacklustre? or are they alive in a way that others aren't?

Enlightenment is the realisation of a fundamental unbroken wholeness. It is the understanding that reality is not to be found in a specific state, experience or location, but is inherent and accessible in all states, experiences and locations.

Reality simply *is*, and whatever is, is reality.

This means that there is nothing to remove, nothing to kill. Our greatest folly is to try and get rid of something which isn't really here in the first place. The sense of self in which we all partake is not an *obstacle* to reality but an *expression* of it.

This sense of self can be compared to waves arising in the ocean. We may first encounter the ocean as a flat calm but it does not remain flat and calm. Soon there are ripples, waves—tsunamis even. Have we now lost the ocean? Shall we search for the water or understand that there is only water?

Your own personality is as rare and beautiful as a star system or an orchid. We are here not just to discover our true Self, but to celebrate, revel and play in the rich deliciousness of our own selfhood, arising out of the boundless silence which embraces all things.

So think or don't think, shout or don't shout, chase enlightenment or cherish your illusions. Everything is welcome here.

Let go or be Dragged

There is a scene in the classic film *Butch Cassidy and the Sundance Kid* which has always struck me as especially relevant to the spiritual path:

The two outlaws have just arrived in Bolivia, keen to go straight and try to find employment as guards for a mining company in the hills. Their potential employer, Percy Garris, challenges Sundance (the fastest draw in the West) to shoot a matchbox lying in the dust some 20 feet away. Sundance accepts, taking his gunslinger's stance, spinning his pistols from his holsters and sizing up the target.

But Garris tells the outlaw that he just wants to know if he can shoot and doesn't need to see anything fancy. And so, counter to his own intuitive and fluid style, Sundance stands still, carefully aims his pistol at the target—and misses.

"Can I move?" He asks over his shoulder.

"What the hell do you mean 'move?'" replies Garris, at which Sundance suddenly ducks and draws, shooting from the hip and obliterating the matchbox with a couple of lightning shots.

"I'm better when I move," says Sundance.

Like Sundance, we are all better when we move with life, rather than clash against its momentum. The freedom we seek is not necessarily the freedom from thoughts, emotions and circumstances, but the capacity to navigate them successfully. It's when we fixate on certain ways of seeing and being that we stall, becoming stuck in our preferences rather than meeting the unfolding moment as it actually is. Living in this way our lives become battlegrounds where our personal expectations are pitted against our real-time sensory experience.

The hard and stiff will be broken, says the *Tao Te Ching. The soft and supple will prevail.* This applies to our inner world of attitudes and perspectives as much as it applies to the external world of objects. If we cannot move with the changing nature of our lives, then we will continue to struggle because life is change and all things are always in a state of transformation.

We may not mind this current of change when it happens to meet our preferences, then we are happy, we can relax. It's only when life rips our best-laid plans to pieces that we feel angry, lost or helpless. We love creation but try our very best to ignore and avoid the inevitable destruction which accompanies it.

The universe is a process of creation and destruction. As you read these words everything around you and within you is being destroyed and recreated. New suns are forming in the depths of space and old suns are shrinking into white dwarfs, or exploding into supernovae. The earth is spinning, shifting and shaking, transforming itself through volcanic activity, earthquakes, landslides and floods. Mount Everest is growing by millimetres and the Moon is drifting away from us by inches.

Life is not the solid and stable experience we imagine it to be. It is a process of continuous transformation, not something we can tame, frame or fix within conceptual paradigms. Life is not a thing. It is an activity. The word 'universe' itself comes for the Latin for *one movement*, an all-encompassing motion from which nothing can possibly stand apart.

There is no you *and* the universe. There is only *the universe* expressing as you, the tree and the Horsehead Nebula. It's a cosmic dance, not a fixed and dead thing.

If the nature of the universe is activity, then it must be our nature too. We are also movement, activity and transformation. Even this body is just another universal process, it is not an end in itself, but a fleeting phase of a movement that has no beginning or end. The word 'process' comes from the Latin *to go forward* and we can feel this flow when we focus on our breathing, heartbeat or the tingling sensations in our hands and feet. You may have noticed the exquisite physical stillness of sitting meditation, but have you noticed how incredibly *alive* that stillness is?

To experience yourself and the world around you

as movement can be profoundly liberating. The walls are not stuck in time, they are dancing. The rocks are not solid, they are transforming. We are not fixed, we are flowing. And this movement is not something that the mind controls; the mind itself is part of this movement. Our thoughts and feelings are the fleeting gestures of a profound cosmic ballet.

"Can I move?" asks Sundance, but the real question is not can we move—we are movement, process, flow. The real question is why don't we feel it? Why do we habitually conceive ourselves as fixed? Why do we cling to our preferences and self-imposed limitations?

Let go, say the Zen Buddhists, *or be dragged.*

Real Magic

I was once lucky enough to come face to face with a real magician. Not a stage magician who pulled rabbits from top hats, but a man who had devoted his entire life to the practice of *Magick*, the esoteric art of influencing the world around us. I was admittedly sceptical of this elderly man who stood all alone, quietly stirring a cup of tea and so asked him point-blank if indeed he was a real magician.

"Aren't we all?" Was his soft reply.

If we really are the magicians of our lives, then we rarely feel like it. We tend to feel powerless rather than all-powerful and there are moments when we feel small, helpless and insignificant. When we imagine the vast expanse of time which existed before our birth and the aeons stretching out after our deaths, our tiny lives seem like flashes in eternity.

We encounter our insignificance when we stare up at the stars on a clear night or gaze at towering mountain ranges. This can be overwhelming, but it can also be an invitation to humility, grace and gratitude. Our culture encourages us to make something of ourselves, to be somebody, to be famous, but this endless striving to arrive somewhere just masks the fact that really we are nothing at all.

Yet it is through this feeling of meaninglessness—an experience which I suggest is purely human—that we can discover depths of meaning, empowerment and even magic.

Let me illustrate this with an analogy. Imagine for a moment that you are standing on the banks of a mighty river, watching the water flowing past you. Your tiny body is nothing compared to this torrent which could easily sweep you away as it carves itself deeper and deeper into the yielding landscape.

But what would happen if you were to crouch down and place your finger into the water? This simple action would have an immediate and observable effect. The water would part around your finger creating a brand-new pattern and rhythm in the river. The pattern may be small and subtle but its effect is undeniable.

This new addition to the water begins to influence the larger flow of the river downstream. If you remove your finger then the effect stops. Put it back in and you potentially alter the entire river, changing its onward journey and expression in ways you cannot control or imagine.

This is why no action—however seemingly small or insignificant—is ever wasted. Everything you think, say and do contributes a new pattern to the river of life and even the smallest addition creates an overall effect.

Now let's change the analogy. Imagine that you

are one of the waves arising in the river. You are a movement of the river itself which, although fleeting, makes and creates part of the ongoing flow. Without you—the wave—the river would express itself differently. There is a saying in the *Kabbalah* that *God needs man as much as man needs God* and it's the same with the river of life.

If there were no waves then there would be no river, and without the river, there can be no waves. Rather than being distinct and separate, wave, river, life, God and individual all rely on each other to exist.

We might feel that we have arrived at this moment through our own willpower, but this would ignore everything that happened upstream. This very moment of your life is the inevitable and impersonal consequence of an infinite number of previous moments and is the impersonal cause of an infinite number of future moments which will flow downstream to affect lives that are yet to blossom.

There are no individuals in this river, no separate selves. Everything which is happening is a torrent of flowing water.

Even though we may sometimes feel helpless or small, we can never be insignificant. Our insignificance is an impossibility. We may judge which of our thoughts and actions have more or less value, but the truth is that everything we do is an act of creation that has an observable and instantaneous effect.

We may not believe in magic but—as the elderly mage implied—we are casting spells in every moment. Every stone we throw creates a ripple. This is a universal law and it is the ordinary magic we share with all men and women. There are few who know this.

Without you, there would be no one to see the sun or the moon. There would be no one to hear laughter or feel joy, pain or fear. Without you, there would be no stars in the night sky, no towering mountain ranges and no endless universe. Without you, there would be nothing at all.

It is because you *are*, that everything *is*.

Now *that* is real magic.

Sit in the Dark

I have a very important question for you: *have you found it yet?* Not your true nature but your false nature? Not your enlightenment but your *endarkenment?* Your core sense of being unworthy, unlovable, shameful or stupid? Because it's here, buried deep in the very fabric of who and what you believe yourself to be.

But of course, we're not interested in this sense of lack and deficiency and try our very best to ignore it completely. Many spiritual practices are designed to avoid confrontation with our brokenness by promising some kind of blissful attainment awaiting us. We want to move forward and not trudge reluctantly into the deep emotional wounds of the past. We're afraid that if we stop, we'll feel it, and if we feel it, we're dead.

Our meditation practice can then become the perfect hideout. The goal becomes the stillness of no-mind, the thought-free state which is like a 5-star luxury resort compared to the gnawing psychodramas of our own mind. But, when we open our eyes again the momentum flows and we find ourselves dealing with the same limiting beliefs about ourselves, other people and the world.

We need to do something more than simply meditate these long-held beliefs away. If we want to test their validity we need to observe them in action, but of course this is not possible in the state of no-mind, because all thoughts are absent. Instead of holding our beliefs up to the light, they remain buried in the dark.

Mindfulness is beneficial, as it allows us simply to observe our experiences arising and passing away without identifying with them. I have found, though, that we may miss the point: we may learn to view the movements of our psyche—our thoughts and feelings, our joy and grief—from a place that seems frigidly removed from life. There's a cold attention, rather than a warm and joyful integration of our internal landscape into the richer tapestry of who we are. This observational approach is useful, necessary and life-changing but it can lead to a duality or split between us and all the parts of ourselves, which, like neglected children, need to be seen, felt, heard and healed. I have experienced this myself:

I had been practising meditation for over ten years before it became dazzlingly apparent that I was using my practice to escape the raw and unprocessed themes which often commanded my subconscious. Sex and violence, fear, rejection and worthlessness all lived inside of me like a dysfunctional family of outsiders, rejects and troublemakers.

But the more I tried to ignore them the more they would scream at me, often exploding in broad daylight when I least expected it.

*A turning point came during a trip to North India.
I was travelling in a cramped Jeep with other back-
packers and locals through the high-altitude desert of
Ladakh, sitting opposite a young Ladakhi girl, perhaps
only three or four years old, asleep on her father's lap.
At one point he reached down and gently adjusted her
little head as if it were the most precious thing in the
universe, and something deep inside of my heart
cracked open. I sat for the rest of that long journey
hiding in my hands, sobbing uncontrollably and unable
to explain to anyone what had happened.*

This experience showed me that my meditation practice alone was not processing my deeper emotional
material, and over the next few years, I became
increasingly swamped by my subconscious as it fought
its way to the surface.

It became apparent that to release and process the
energy of my subconscious I needed to do something
more than just sit on my meditation cushion in a state
of mindless bliss. I needed to talk to someone and tell
my own story rather than deny that I even had one.
And so I began to see a counsellor and we started to
explore my inner family of troublemakers that I had
been afraid of for so long.

During one of our sessions, I mentioned that I had
recently noticed the sense of a huge, dark, menacing

figure looming over my left shoulder. The moment I spoke about him I realised that he had been with me since childhood. That night as I lay in bed, I felt the presence of this shadowy figure again, and out of sheer curiosity, I spoke to him:

Who are you?

I hate you.

Why do you hate me?

Because you ignore me.

I had no idea that he could talk or had a story of his own. I suddenly understood that he only appeared dark, powerful and menacing because I had forced him to live in the shadows. He didn't want to destroy me, he only wanted to step into the light and be known, just like all the other aspects of myself. I told him:

I don't hate you.

I love you.

You are Me.

I then turned towards this towering dark figure and embraced him. He did not struggle or refuse, he relaxed. As we embraced each other he merged into me and we became one person. I had reached a point in my life where I was able not only to recognise my shadow but speak to it and integrate its energies into a more fulfilling experience of myself.

We meditators are often desperate to ascend into the peace and stillness of the observer state, rather than descend into the murk of our own physical being. But to know ourselves fully, we must be prepared to see and befriend our own darkness. This means sitting with, and talking to, the parts of us which have become hard and frozen, thawing them with the warm sun of Awareness.

Our true nature is discovered not only in the rarified air of transcendence but in the deep dark chasms of our emotions, fears and reactivity. This ordinary body which we try to escape, terrified as we are of its ghosts and feral entities, is also the path home to a fully embodied freedom.

Enlightenment is not the absence of the dark, but the fearless willingness to illuminate the dark.

The View from Nowhere

One day when I was with my young son on Douglas Head, the coastal headland overlooking the town where we live, we stopped to look at a panorama that mapped all of the buildings below. We could find the museum, the theatre and the promenade, but after some time, Leo asked me, "But where are *we*, dad?"

This was a good question. Our location wasn't on the map because it was where we were looking *from*. We transcended the panorama, viewing it from an unmapped vantage point.

It's the same with our experience of ourselves. Where exactly do we locate ourselves in the ever-changing landscape of mind, body and emotions? Have a look now and see if you can find the place where 'you' seem to be. Perhaps you can feel a sense of pressure behind your eyes or face, or a contraction in your head somewhere? Is that you? Or perhaps you are a feeling in the body, a voice in your head or a mental image of yourself? Is that you?

If that is you, then who is looking at that image or sensation? Can you be something you are looking at? When you look in the mirror are you the same as the reflection in the glass?

We cannot be anything that arises in our

panorama (a word from the Greek, meaning *all which is seen*) as we are always observing it, and yet we tend to spend our lifetime identifying with feelings and emotions which are by their nature transient. How many times have we asserted *I am happy* or *I am sad*, essentially equating ourselves with a passing state of mind, a state of mind that is always an *observed* state of mind?

You cannot *be* happy or sad because they are impermanent emotions that arise and fade as a direct consequence of internal and external conditions, all of which are also arising and fading in real time. Because of this, neither happiness, sadness nor any other internal state can last. We experience them, but we cannot be reduced to them.

By identifying ourselves with something in our experience, we suffer, just as identifying myself as one of the buildings in the panorama would cause confusion by forming an identification with something I couldn't possibly be.

But not all languages allow for this mistaken identity with passing phenomena. In Manx Gaelic (the native language of the Isle of Man) you would say *Sadness is on me* rather than *I am sad*.

This way of speaking allows much more freedom in thinking and feeling. Now, sadness is just something that is on you. Happiness is on you, fear is on you, misery is on you. To say that something is *on* you is much different to saying that something *is* you.

If something is on you then it can also be *off* you, like a piece of clothing. You might wear a hat on a cold day but that doesn't mean that you *are* the hat. To say so would be absurd. Wearing the hat has a time limit, you do not wear it forever.

This allows the understanding that states of mind and body come and go and we are not the same as them. These too are happening in the vista of our present-moment experience and our very observation of them indicates that we have automatically transcended them.

Our internal sense of self is also just another feature we can locate and observe, playing itself out as an interactive flow of thought, memory, emotion and sensation.

This is the power of observation. Everything we can observe is precisely what we are not, and *That* which we are, cannot be observed at all.

Unlike our sense of self, our awareness cannot be found because it is beyond every location, it is the space in which all locations appear. That which is aware of the map, cannot itself be mapped. Every time we believe we have found ourselves as an experience of silence, stillness or love, we are in fact observing just another passing feature of the panorama.

This is the discovery of our own placeless awareness, our unborn nature. It is ancient and yet ever-present. It cannot be conceptualised and yet welcomes all concepts. It cannot be seen or heard and yet welcomes all sights and sounds. Each passing moment of the cosmos springs forth from it and then vanishes back into it.

Your effortless awareness has no location, shape or form, no drama, no birth, no death and no problem. It's where you are always looking from, hearing from, experiencing from.

Even if you see the light, know that you are beyond the light.

There's Nobody in the Body

There is a Zen story which tells of two princesses wandering a battlefield littered with dead samurai:

> *"Here are the bodies," said one of the princesses, "but where are the people?"*

Often when we hear about the realisation of no-self it becomes just another concept for our busy mind to chew on, but we can have a direct experience of this deep truth by simply dropping away from the mind, and down into the effortless flow of this ancient, wise body.

No-self is not an idea, but an experience. Your own body is the perfect expression of no-self, here and now. From the 7 octillion atoms which make up your current physical form and the 30 trillion bacteria living in your gut, the unique heritage encoded in your DNA, to the microscopic galaxies of life swirling in your cells, to your ever-changing muscles, mind, bones and brain, there is no such thing as a separate self, owner or controller to be found.

This body we refer to as ours, is nothing but the intelligent arrangement of trillions of cells which are operating within you as you read these words. We have no consciousness of their activity and neither do we need to be conscious of them to function in daily life.

Your heart, lungs, nervous system and digestion, immune system and metabolism all function independently of the need for you to manage them consciously. Even your balance—when you get up in the middle of the night, half-asleep, to go to the bathroom there is an intelligence at work which prevents you from immediately falling over.

Even if we were to slice ourselves into millions of pieces we would still not find the separate solid self we believe lives 'in here'. We can find thoughts and feelings about being a separate self (this is *my* mind, *my* body, *my* pain) but we cannot find the actual self to which these experiences refer.

Here is the body but where is the person? We spend much of our lives referring back to something which does not exist.

Just reflect for a moment: do your heart or stomach contain a separate self? Is there an ego in your bones or skin? Did you have to contribute a single thought for your hands and feet (with all of their sensitivity and dexterity) to take form?

This is a radical discovery: our ship has no captain and yet instinctively it knows how to sail. With every step we take or cup of coffee we drink, there is an intelligence acting through us which the mind cannot fully comprehend. If the mind were to suddenly awaken to it, it would realise that, like a child steering a rocket-ship ride at the fairground, it has never been the true pilot.

But this selfless intelligence is not unique to us, it is the essence of all nature. The apple tree has no self to produce apples and the wave needs no owner to arise and pass. The clouds, rivers and mountains are utterly empty of personal volition or choice—yet we cannot deny their beauty.

When the sun shines on our faces it is not a reward, it's just nature. When the rain soaks us to the skin it's not a punishment, it's just nature. The thoughts we experience, the sounds we hear and the feelings we feel, are also just nature. They neither contain a separate self nor do they occur to a separate self. The truth is that from our heads to our toes we have always been absolutely devoid of a solid self and yet so paradoxically full of a deeply embodied intelligence that already knows how to laugh, grieve and cry, live, transform and die.

You Are Flying

Haven't we all tried to fly as children? I can remember climbing onto the arm of the sofa one Christmas, wearing in my new Superman pyjamas and launching myself into the air, rejoicing in the thrill of flight just for a moment.

But flying isn't just for superheroes. In spiritual traditions, we also find heroes of consciousness who can perform superhuman feats. In ancient Tibetan Buddhist texts there exist stories of yogis and yoginis who could miraculously glide through the open sky.

This may be a long-forgotten form of self-mastery or simply an exciting metaphor for liberation, but there really is a way that we can all experience the joy of flight, and it's much easier than we imagine.

We can recognise the ephemeral nature of experience. Although we refer to our everyday waking state as 'real life' not a single second of it can be paused, held or put in our pocket. Real life is made entirely from moments that are insubstantial and fleeting. Every night since birth the waking state itself has faded away as we fall asleep and enter the dream state. Just as in the waking state, our dreams feel real when we are in them, but they too melt away and we cannot hold on even to our most pleasant dreams. The dream-state too fades away exposing deep dreamless sleep, an oblivion in which there is no sense of self or world. If someone were to offer us £1,000,000 just to say our name in this state, we would be unable to. Finally, after a period of time in deep sleep, we wake up again and open our eyes to the 'real world', forgetting that this world has a time limit to it.

But which of these transient states is real? Although we assert that one of these states is reality, and the others aren't, the truth is that waking, dreaming and deep sleep are all equally ephemeral. They have the appearance of reality but lack any substance.

This fundamental lack of solidity may feel alarming, but it means that right now, we and all things are already free. In fact, there is only freedom. All things in all states are already ungrounded and unbounded.

So whether you are working, dreaming or dissolved in deep sleep, you are always experiencing the dream-like nature of consciousness. There is no solid ground beneath you or a fixed world around us. There is only the endless play of emptiness appearing and disappearing as a multitude of formless forms.

This profound emptiness means that you are already airborne. You are already gliding through the appearance of each empty moment.

Just notice how each passing state moves through you—effortlessly. Without donning a Superman costume see how your perceptions stream past you like clouds through the sky. Without leaving your chair, observe how you fly through the empty space of each moment, like a bird gliding through the wide and open sky.

In all states and in all directions, there is only liberation. Every iota of experience is free-floating, dreamlike and traceless. Past, present and future: there has never been any solid ground.

So sit back, relax and enjoy your flight…!

Everybody has Your Face

What would it be like to be somebody else for the day? Not just those that we admire or envy, but our spiritual heroes? The enlightened saints, masters and mystics we often look towards for our daily inspiration? What would it be like if I were you, and you were me?

It is remarkably simple to have a felt sense of being another person because we all share the same name. Our given name might be Mike, Bill or Sarah but we all refer to ourselves as *I*. This is our inner name which signifies the fact that we exist. To say *I* is to admit *I am aware*.

We all share in and partake of this core awareness. Yes, the contents of my own subjective experience at this moment will be different to yours, but the awareness is the same. I know that I exist just as you know that you exist.

This means that if we want to taste another person's subjectivity we only have to stop and rest in our own. It's this ordinary subjectivity that unifies us with all human beings, past, present and future. It's the doorway to Oneness, beyond individuality.

Understand that your own *I am* is the very same *I am* of everyone around you. Can you see that those around you also share this simple experience of being aware? Of knowing that they exist?

Now try bringing someone to mind and imagine that this person is sitting here instead of you. Actually, this person *is* you, just another you. Let yourself simply be this person for a few moments, as if they were having this particular experience. Can you notice that their experience of being aware is the same as your own experience of being aware?

This is what it feels like to be this person. To know them as they know themselves. Allow yourself to rest as them for a while.

You can try this practice with other people in your life, perhaps bringing to mind a loved one, a stranger, a troublemaker or spiritual teacher. Can you see that you share an inherent commonality with all these people just as they share it with you?

The experience of another person is also the experience of yourself. It is the simple experience of being aware. There is no extra holiness or wisdom, no special knowledge or cosmic state of mind, there's just the basic awareness that has illuminated the minds, bodies and worlds of everyone from our cave-dwelling ancestors to astronauts, saints and sinners, lovers and strangers.

The awareness to which we refer when we say *I am* is what 'en-lightens' (or illuminates) our experience, moment after moment. This natural and effortless knowing is what the thinking mind mythologises as an objective experience. The mind then searches for this same knowing as a future achievement to be attained at the feet of a guru, or through decades of esoteric meditation practice. And yet the truth is that the real guru is always present as our own silent awareness. If we seek outwardly for it then we turn away from our own obvious light source and home ground.

But if we are all (already) en-lightened from the same unified source, then what creates the difference between the sages of the world and its tyrants, bullies and dictators? Well, it is a matter of what we add to ourselves and what we take away.

The power-hungry seek to accumulate more and more, weighing themselves down with thoughts and beliefs, identities, goals and possessions. They cripple themselves with past and future, gain and loss, whilst desperately trying to master an ever-shifting universe that is continuously slipping through their fingers.

The sages travel light: they do not add weight to themselves but reduce, detach and subtract. They release their attachment to mind, body and world, seeing that these are insubstantial and dream-like. They stop asking their minds for answers a mind cannot give.

Yes, they let go—but they do not fall.

It is everything else that falls away, revealing its transient nature. What is ever-present is the effortless awareness which illuminates all things from the dewdrop to the constellation of Ursa Major. This is the eternal inner sun of radiant awareness.

Those in love with the mind smother themselves with names and forms, whereas those in love with God boil themselves dry until only God remains.

But accumulation is a habit of the mind and we have all forgotten the simple and radical freedom of resting as awareness—as *I am*—without imprisoning ourselves within a cage of adjectives.

To counter this outward grasping, we can step back consciously into the nakedness of our own being and recognise that, despite our apparent differences, we all share the same name, the same being, the same true face. The imagined gulf between us and the enlightened masters can then evaporate as we understand that the light they speak from, is the light we are.

The truth is that you have only ever seen your light. Your own, wondrous light.

Kiss the Frog

I vividly recall the moment when my attitude to pain transformed. It was day 6 of a 10-day meditation retreat and I was in agony. Sitting cross-legged on a cushion in the packed meditation hall, my spine burned and my legs were as numb as concrete slabs. I was beginning to realise that even sitting still in a dharma centre, in the middle of the tranquil countryside, pain was inevitable.

Something deep inside my right hip joint was smouldering, becoming increasingly hot and spreading outwards like an all-consuming fire. This pain was too much to bear and as I tried my best to sit as still as one of the bronze Buddhas which decorated the room, it seemed as though everyone around me was also struggling. I could hear the sighs and clumsy shifting sounds of my fellow meditators as they changed posture, heaving their numbed legs, like heavy logs, into a new arrangement.

Despite my pain, I was intent on keeping still. To move was to fail. To be overtaken with pain was to lose equanimity. And yet as the sensation in my hip increased to a white-hot pain, I finally conceded and told myself that if I didn't move now, I might damage myself in the long term. I had tried my very best to block out my pain, and it had won. Just as I was about to move, I remembered something the teacher had told us at the very start of the retreat. He said that before moving away from pain, focus into it and see if you can find its centre. I had not tried this, and so I diligently focused all my attention down into the flames engulfing my hip joint. Suddenly I found something: a quick and heavy pulsation right in the middle of the pain. I had not noticed this before and realised that it must be a nerve. This was where the pain was emanating from. I had found it!

Then something extraordinary happened: the pain stopped. It dropped from 100 to 0 in a split second. I was still focusing into my hip joint, but now there was only the soft tingling buzz of neutral sensation. *Where had the pain gone?* I asked myself in astonishment, *and was it really there in the first place?*

For the first time in my life, I had chosen to focus into the heart of a painful experience, rather than ignore it and the effect was transformational. Perhaps this is why traditions such as Buddhism emphasise suffering as an inherent part of life. Sickness, old age and death are not exactly what we want to hear when we encounter the Buddha's teachings, but neither can we completely ignore the fact that these uncomfortable experiences are inevitable for us all, enlightened or not.

Our usual reactivity to pain and discomfort reveals

how we tend to battle against the body's behaviours when it stops meeting our expectations. We struggle because we do not consciously choose these experiences and yet once they arrive, we often have no choice but to admit their disruptive presence.

The practice of *being with* discomfort is always counterintuitive. It's a skill that requires time to cultivate as we develop our capacity to *be with* the ebb and flow of this human body. We don't have to like everything that arises, but we do have to accept it because it is already here and no amount of imagination can make it disappear. Trying to resist what is already happening seems like it might just work, but it only adds extra weight to our suffering.

But what if we could encounter our pain and illness consciously, attentively, with acceptance and curiosity? If we cannot completely avoid them, the least we can do is to become more skilled at working with them whenever they arise. This means that we no longer wait—or brace ourselves—for discomfort to arise, but actively seek ways in which we can encounter and become familiar with it.

We can explore leaning into discomfort on purpose. Whether it is spending time resting inside a feeling of pain or sadness, fasting or taking cold showers. The great secret of life is that if we relax, it relaxes too.

Something remarkable can happen when we are

brave enough to encounter our pain and discomfort: these apparently toxic experiences can transmute into medicine. The more we can make space for our discomfort, without reacting against it or trying to block it out, the more room it has to shift, soften and relax, often transforming before our very eyes.

This is an act of compassion. We are bearing witness to ourselves, being present within our pain and suffering. The more we can feel into our own rawness, our own contraction and pain, the better able we are to be fully present with somebody else's. We don't have to fix them or stop their pain and sadness; we can be *with* them without division, in this particular moment of the expanding universe.

Sickness, depression and sadness are never dead ends or wrong turns but gateways to wisdom, interconnection and freedom. If you were able to banish all your suffering and hardship right now then you would also be ridding yourself of all your potential wisdom, insight and service. The world does not need teachers who have never felt the depths of despair, but people who have sat with their suffering and found the light.

But we know this already, don't we? The fairy tales we hear as children are full of reminders that appearances can be deceptive, and that conscious intimacy with suffering can lead to personal transformation. I have always thought the story of the *Frog Prince* illustrates this particularly well:

A beautiful young princess is playing with her favourite toy, a golden ball, when she accidentally drops it into a deep, dark well. She is distraught until a frog emerges with the golden ball, asking if they can be friends. The princess reluctantly agrees, and although she is initially disgusted by the appearance of this slimy, warty amphibian, she allows it to accompany her back to the palace. As time passes her aversion to the frog begins to fade and she begins to enjoy his company, allowing him to eat from her plate, and even sleep on her pillow.

One day the frog announces that his appearance is not his true form. He is in fact a handsome prince under a spell cast by a wicked witch. If she would kiss him on his lips the spell would be lifted and he would be transformed. So, she kisses him and it is this act of trust and intimacy that changes the frog into the prince, which is ultimately what every princess is searching for.

The message is that if we can muster the energy, trust and courage to caress and hold whatever repulses us, then we can heal ourselves, bringing exiled feelings and emotions home to a larger sense of being. This in turn transforms the ways in which we encounter the world, which is always a world of change, a world of turbulence. We can become skilled at allowing the many flavours of the human experience to arise and fall within us, like ever-cresting waves without being overwhelmed by them.

Old age, sickness and death then become much more than inconveniences. They reveal themselves as golden opportunities to live happily ever after.

Observe Yourself: the sword of awareness

It's not just that we are alive that is miraculous, but that our lives contain so much potential. We are the only species on earth with the ability to observe—and therefore question—our own mental worlds. Mindfulness is a practice which enables us to step back and untangle ourselves from the sticky web of our conditioning.

It has taken millions of years for our species to evolve into its current form, but through the practice of self-observation we can evolve psychologically within the span of a single lifetime.

This is why our practice is so vital. Observation is the key to transformation and because no one else has access to our inner world it falls to us alone to cultivate the traits of the wise person. We do this by sitting with our present-moment experience, watching our minds reflect back to us the dynamic content of our lives. The thoughts, reactions and desires which bubble up into consciousness are never random, but reveal the very tapestry of our own unique conditioning. We are watching ourselves happen in real time.

There is wisdom in this watching. By stepping back and observing our personal content arise and pass, like cloud formations through the sky, we can allow everything to come and go, celebrating the richness of our experience, without becoming captured by it. We watch the clouds without getting lost in the clouds.

The goal of self-observation is not somehow to extinguish our unique conditioning—it is not 'ours' to extinguish—but simply to observe it from a place of awareness, with equanimity. Whereas the *mind* may squirm at some of its own content, our *awareness* is always impartial, illuminating both the thought and the reaction to it.

We deprogramme ourselves to the extent that we can observe the programme. The programme itself is neither good nor bad, it is merely a pattern of nature with which we have identified and fuelled through decades of repetition.

The programme we call *me* is never actually our own. We did not choose it, we cannot control it and we cannot stop it. We did not choose to be born to these particular parents, with this particular DNA, in this particular culture, time and place.

All of us have an immense potential to grow psychologically and yet we spend much of our lives repeating patterns of action and reaction that we have never consciously chosen.

Only when we see this pattern can we deviate from it. Seeing the pattern is almost like making a wish in a fairy tale because we are given something new: the prospect of choice. This is the shift from thought to awareness, from unconsciousness to consciousness, from ignorance to wisdom, and has significant implications for us and for others.

The more we disentangle ourselves from our own limiting patterns, the more we can be of genuine service to others. Through observing our own minds, bodies and emotions we come to understand, to know intuitively, the minds, bodies and emotions of all people, everywhere,

By knowing yourself, you know everyone else too. This allows for a natural sense of friendship and compassion in our connections with the people around us. We have enhanced abilities to be of service to them so that they too can navigate their own inner worlds. The word compassion means to 'feel with' so that when we are moved to help it's from a place of intuitive fellowship and equality. We are not offering service to lowly others from a lofty, superior perspective, instead we are discovering that there are no others.

But it's not only humans who benefit from our practice of self-observation. None of the other 8.7 million species of life inhabiting the earth can serve the planet as well as we can. We are the only species that possesses a consciousness, which can understand and serve all other life forms. We are the only beings that can choose to *love* all other beings.

This makes us very special indeed.

But living enmeshed with our conditioning we lack the perspective to question our current relationship with life. You cannot wake another person from their nightmare if you are still absorbed in your own. Living in this way there is very little which separates us from the other species to which we often feel so superior. Without wisdom, without observation, there can be little humanity, only a small bundle of conditioning living a fearful life.

It is a great tragedy that we humans are so very close to activating our true potential, and yet so very far, too.

If we want to evolve consciously and serve others, we must cut ourselves free from the thorny briars of our conditioning. For that, a special weapon is required—a weapon that can cut through the tangles of unconsciousness, a weapon that we all inherit and yet is so rarely unsheathed. This is the weapon of self-observation.

The legend of King Arthur and the Sword in the Stone illustrates the transformative consequence of wielding this weapon.

The story tells us that young Arthur must pull the sword, Excalibur, from the stone to claim his heritage as King of England. This powerful sword imbued with mystical powers represents our inherent ability to observe and cut through the tangles of our own conditioning. Such awareness is synonymous with freedom, because if we do not recognise our habits and patterns, we have no choice but to act upon them.

But Excalibur—the sword of light—is buried up to its hilt in stone. It is stuck, and whilst it is stuck it is useless. In fact, it is we who have become petrified, merged with our thoughts and unable to perceive the clarity and beauty of each new moment. Without this weapon, we cannot think, feel, or respond outside of our tight conditioning. If we are to wake up and serve, the sword of light, which is also the sword of awareness, must be retrieved.

But who can do that? Can somebody else be aware for you? Can your teacher or guru observe the subtleties of your own mental world? The legend tells us that only the true king can pull Excalibur from the stone. This king is of course ourselves, our true Self—silent, spacious and ever-present.

When we step back from our programming and sit on the throne of awareness, the seat of the Self, then we take our rightful place as the wise ruler and benevolent overseer of our experience, rather than its suffering slave. Does the king serve the servants?

Once pulled free this sword will cut through anything it strikes. All thoughts, emotions, habits, patterns, identities and beliefs, wilt and die when struck by its keen, bright blade. This is the magic to which we all have access. The magic of self-observation.

So often we are waiting for somebody else to retrieve this sword for us. We imagine that only a spiritual master or enlightened teacher could possibly assist our growth, happiness or wellbeing. We have no idea just how powerful we are.

Only you can transform yourself because only you can observe yourself. This is wisdom at work. It is how we cut ourselves, and all others free.

Excalibur is in your hands.

You Are Everything

"Michael—do you want to see a ghost?"

My grandfather slid the photograph across the table towards me and I winced in anticipation of seeing the nightmarish figure glaring back at me. My grandparents had recently arranged a family gathering in one of our island's beautiful glens and had photographed the occasion. It was only when the film was developed that they realised that there was a mysterious intruder standing at the back, next to my cousins. The ghostly figure has a strange, twisted face that seemed to be laughing, or perhaps grimacing at the camera.

At least this was what my grandfather told me one evening over the phone. I had always been fascinated by the supernatural and so the next time I visited them I immediately asked to see this inexplicable picture. My grandmother found the image so unsettling that she left the room. I held the picture in my hands staring at the image and waiting for the shock of seeing an apparition gazing back at me. I looked again, scanning the faces of my cousins, aunties and uncles. Still nothing. Finally, I asked my grandfather where the ghost was and he immediately jabbed his finger at the back row "There!" he cried, incredulous that I could somehow miss this proof of the spirit world.

"You mean, Uncle Robert?"

"What?" He replied, snatching the picture and fixing his glasses to concentrate on the strange face in front of him.

"That's Uncle Robert, Grandad."

Sure enough, the 'ghost' was none other than my uncle. Yes, the camera had caught him with a strange smile and there was an odd, dappled effect of the sunlight on his face, but it was only my uncle in the picture and not a ghost.

Sometimes it is easy to miss what is in front of us if we are looking for something else. In the middle of the night, the coat hanging on the back of the door becomes a bogeyman, a family member in a photograph becomes a phantom. We see what we believe or misinterpret, not what is actually there.

My grandfather asked me if I wanted to see a ghost but I want to ask you a question:

Do you want to see God?

Do you want to see Brahman, the Dao, Reality, with your own eyes?

Would you believe me if I told you that the reality we search for is nothing other than our own experience, here and now? And that far from being hidden, it is the most obvious, direct and available experience we have. In fact, it's all we have ever experienced.

But there is a catch: we constantly miss reality because it permeates our experience so thoroughly. We believe the world to be something else, something mundane, something standing in the way of reality. We don't want the ordinary world, we want a mystical state of mind, not understanding that every state of mind is mystical. So, like the fish looking for water while it swims in the sea, the reason we can't find God is because it's all there is and could possibly be.

This is the deep and direct teaching which can be found at the heart of the world's wisdom traditions: *all is one and the one is all.* This total unwavering unity means that there is nothing extra we must do to 'gain' reality, there is only something to see. This is already the eternal moment and it looks and feels and tastes exactly like this. It has no centre, no edge. It is neither personal nor impersonal. Everything arises from it and subsides back into it again.

Can we see this moment, this world, this life as it really is and not veil it with the belief that happiness, freedom, enlightenment and God are somewhere else? Are you ready to hear that all is one, despite the appearances of multiplicity? Can you accept that there is nowhere to get to, other than this miraculous moment?

Now he is all. There is nothing distinct from himself
[...] this is the state of Brahman.
This is the state of natural presence.
You are that true state.

So says the *Ellam Ondre* the anonymous Tamil scrip-
ture, which the great 20th Century Hindu sage, Sri
Ramana Maharshi recommended to his devotees.

Intellectually it may sound so simple and yet our
beliefs about life act as thick towering walls against
reality. We live behind those metaphorical walls in a
citadel of our own making: to see everything as God
would mean the end of our limitation. Even when I
pointed out to my grandfather that the 'ghost' was his
very-much-alive son staring back at him, it still took
him another few minutes to check its truth.

For those of us who want more than mere words,
perhaps an analogy can help. If we must awaken to our
true nature as reality then in some sense we must be
asleep. We are dreaming of ourselves as a solid separate
self, negotiating a solid separate world and taking this
dream to be the hard truth. Awakening does not
require us to somehow stop the dream from continuing
but to understand that it is nothing more than a dream.

And what is the nature of this dream? What is the
nature of any dream? A dream is an appearance that
seems to be real but dissolves upon inspection. A
dream is not the hard truth. It is transient and

fleeting, it morphs and changes. Like an illusion or a mirage, it cannot be grasped or solidified.

But there is another aspect to our dreams which can be useful to appreciate, especially if we want to see God as everything. Consider that every single dream you have ever had, whether it was blissful or terrifying, lucid or opaque, was nothing other than a projection of your own creative mind.

Everyone you have ever met in a dream, and every-thing you have ever done in a dream has only been an expression of your mind's infinitely creative activity. Allow a few moments for that realisation to sink in— all you have ever experienced in your dreams is your own mind. *Your mind as the dream.*

Now let's try something. Have a good look around the room you are in. Notice your surroundings, the walls and floor, tables and chairs, trees or mountains. Just be interested in them for a few moments before continuing. Read the next part carefully:

Just as in your dreams, everything you are looking at right now is also nothing but your own mind.
Your mind as this.

Everything you are experiencing at this moment is an appearance of yourself. There is no separate self *in here* and no external world *out there*. Nothing stands separate from you, everything arises inside you, inside your own awareness.

You are everything, and this *everything-ness* is nothing in particular. It's a flow of mind, a flow of awareness, a flow of God.

There was never a small separate mind inside which we lived. There has only ever been the one mind, the non-dual nature of God. If you can glimpse this for even a moment then the small self which yearns for a future enlightenment can fall away, allowing the full glory of reality to flood in.

Despite all our seeking, we have never taken a single step away from reality. Can God take a step away from God? We have always had the world inside us, unified with the stars and planets, animals and people, mountains and deserts, thoughts, feelings and actions.

The very thing we have been looking for has always been here, right from the very start, just waiting—quietly, patiently—for a moment of recognition in which we finally see that all is One. For as the great Sufi mystic Ibn Arabi reminds us,

You see him[2]
But you do not know
You see him.

Well, now you know.

---

2. Twinch, C (trans.) Ibn Arabi / Balyani, 2011. *Know Yourself: an explanation of the oneness of being.* Beshara Publications, Cheltenham

Be Still and Know Nothing

Can you imagine spending your whole life searching for something that you can never find? Saint Thomas Aquinas was a respected philosopher and theologian, the pinnacle of whose life work was the treatise, *Summa Theologica*. He had a mystical experience in 1273 CE, in which he realised that, "All that I have written seems like straw compared to what has now been revealed to me." He put down the *Summa Theologica* from that moment.

Such experiences of seeking and finding, contraction and expansion are unavoidable on the spiritual path. For example, Sri Nisargadatta Maharaj, the great 20th-century *jnani* who taught from his small attic room in Mumbai, said in his final talks:

> *Whatever I had thought earlier has now changed. What is happening now is that even the slightest touch of individuality has completely disappeared, and it is consciousness as such which is spontaneously experiencing. The result is total freedom.*[3]

Today's Enlightenment is tomorrow's mistake say the Zen Buddhists. I know well, from my own experience, the

3. Dunn, J, 1994. *Conscousness and the Absolute: The Final Talks of Sri Nisargadatta Maharaj.* Acorn Press, Durham, NC.

agonising confusion of absolute certainty suddenly reduced to the cold ashes of doubt. But it is important to understand that the purpose of the spiritual journey isn't to achieve something or know something special that nobody else knows. It is a wrecking ball, designed to destroy all of our certainties, cherished opinions and fixed ideas. It's a return to naked unknowing, to living life as zero.

It is zero that contains all the potential.

In the months after awakening, my practices fell away because I understood that the person who had meditated every day to achieve enlightenment in the future, had never really existed in the first place. There was no need to go looking for reality when there was only reality.

But as the years passed I noticed that this realisation which had felt like the ultimate full stop, was actually just another comma and new insights began to emerge spontaneously which made my previous certainties seem laughable.

I declared myself finished, done and free, yet each day brought with it entirely new ways of seeing myself and the world which was inaccessible only weeks earlier. Slowly, reluctantly, I began to see that I had been wrong. There is no such thing as enlightenment—only an endless process of *enlightenments.*

Awakening is the end of our identity as a solid, time-bound separate self, and yet it's just the very start of knowing ourselves as something endless and nameless. If we believe that we have understood something special, or become someone special, then we have fallen asleep again. We have formed a new identity, a new story and become stuck once again, missing a brand-new moment of the universe about which the mind knows absolutely nothing.

The truth is that even our most life-changing insights change and mature over time, revealing ever more subtlety and flavour. If we don't appreciate this, then we run the risk—and it is a real risk—of trying to form an identity from those insights. Such an identity gets stuck back in time; it's no longer true, fresh and relevant and the exquisite taste of those delicious early insights is lost.

What is enlightenment then? It is not what we imagine it to be, and it *cannot* be imagined. It's not a single *blitzkrieg* of unassailable mystical knowledge, but simply the end of searching for ourselves in the ever-changing contents of mind, body and world. We have no identity because, in essence, we are nothing.

Yet, enlightenment is the start of a new adventure into limitless terrain and for this we must surrender all of our accumulated knowledge and assumptions. None of that is useful as we stand on the edge of an unfolding reality. As with the parable of the blind men and the elephant let's not trap ourselves by glimpsing the tail or the trunk and declaring that we have now found a definitive description of the complete truth.

We can use our practice to stay wide open, resting in a child-like mind, a 'beginner's mind,[4]' a zero mind. We allow insights, realisations and epiphanies to come and go through our own silent spacious being, knowing them, savouring them, but not fixating on any particular flash as the final truth. We stand naked and ready for the next ordinary moment to reveal the unprecedented nature of reality.

Doubt does not stand in the way of truth, it's a *flavour* of truth. The doubt which throws us into confusion is holy and cleansing. For something new to be built the ground must first be cleared. The nature of the universe is creation and destruction, birth and death, but this is also the nature of understanding. It is humbling to know that the unshakeable enlightenment we may claim to have can be demolished by the very next moment. It means that ultimately we can say or know nothing with absolute conviction and it's absolute conviction that will imprison us. Only through this small and quivering droplet of consciousness can we attempt to determine the nature of things, who we are and what we are not, and yet this is always enough. It's enough to know that we don't know, then the gate is wide open. The question is:

---

4. Suzuki, S. 2011. *Zen Mind, Beginner's Mind: Informal Talks on Zen Meditation and Practice.* Shambhala Publications Inc., Boulder, CO.

Are you willing to surrender?
To start again? To be no-one?
Will you happily trade your well-earned penny of knowledge for the eternal mystery?

Everything else, my friends, is a *mere straw*.

Your Final Breath

Last night I stopped breathing. I suddenly woke in the middle of the night with a surge of adrenaline, violently gasping for my next breath. The one thing I had spent so many years focusing on in my meditation practice, the natural and effortless process I had completely taken for granted, had just stopped.

Stumbling blindly around my bedroom, my eyes, nose and throat burning, I tried to inhale with every ounce of mental and physical energy, but my throat was blocked shut. All my meditation practices, insight and spiritual experiences were useless and unavailable. My only thought was *Breathe! Breathe!*

After 4 or 5 almost impossible breaths my wife awoke, leapt out of bed and began thumping my back. I slumped down against the bed with my head between my knees and something gurgled in my belly and chest, finally clearing the blockage.

I have never in my life taken breaths as sweet, nourishing and needed as the ones which followed, and soon I was able to calm down, climb back into bed and slowly fall back to sleep.

This incident was nothing. It may have only lasted 10 or 15 seconds. I did not collapse and I did not end up in hospital. But it was enough to remind me not to take my life for granted. If I had been alone then who knows what could have happened?

This morning, life feels wonderful and new. It has a lustre which wasn't there before. Each breath—slow and deep—now feels like a luxury, like golden life-giving nectar flooding into me and opening me up. I can notice the subtle physical joy of each inhalation and the deep release of each exhalation.

We only wake up to how much we truly love our lives when our most essential and life-giving functions falter. The truth is that life is breath and breath is life. When it stops, we stop.

Even if we survive a series of false alarms and near misses, eventually our heart will stop beating, illness or disease will overrun our faltering immune system.

This message of fragility, transience and vulnerability is contradicted by teachings about power and eternity. Far from being reminded of our vulnerability, we are told that we are beyond the mind and body, birth and death. We are *Brahman*, pure awareness unbesmirched by the grit and grime of the world.

Powerful as this message is, there is another realisation I hold equally valuable. Yes, we are ultimately unfindable, beyond mind and body and the world, and yet completely and utterly vulnerable.

How can these apparent opposites melt together? Well, isn't it beautiful that they do? We are infinite awareness and simultaneously just one breath away from non-existence.

Zen traditions emphasise the power of our vulnerability to awaken powerful wisdom. It is only through acknowledging and embracing our own human fragility that we access wisdom, compassion and interconnection.

We all share this vulnerability. You don't need to wait to become enlightened or have a spiritual experience. This fundamental knowledge of our own fragility is the balm that allows us to connect to everyone who has ever lived and everyone who is yet to live.

Feeling vulnerable can often be an isolating experience, as we sit with our pain, fear, depression or loneliness, but we often forget that we are also sitting with something very human, which we all feel at some point. It connects us with all possible people from all possible times.

There is a Zen story that reflects this:

Zen Master Ryokan was asked by his family to help with their nephew who was causing scandal by running around town spending money on courtesans. They thought a few wise words from his Buddhist uncle may help him see sense. So Ryokan, an elderly man, makes the long journey to see his nephew and when he arrives his nephew is glad to see him again and asks him to stay the night.

They spend time together talking, but Ryokan

does not mention the value of meditation or the teachings of the Buddha. Finally, the young nephew goes to sleep and Ryokan stays awake all night, meditating.

In the morning when they part, Ryokan bends down to put his sandals on and notices that his hands are shaking, "I must be getting old," he says, "would you mind tying my laces for me?" As his nephew ties his old uncle's laces, Ryokan reminds him, "You see, a man grows weaker and more feeble each day. Take good care of yourself."

He did not mention morality, enlightenment or the indestructible nature of his nephew's primordial awakened mind. He simply reminded him that life is precious and should not be taken for granted. The nephew hears the message clearly and becomes reformed.

In this story, Ryokan stays awake all night meditating whilst his young nephew sleeps. He is already an elderly man and perhaps he has not much life left and yet he chooses to spend his evening sitting in meditation. Why? Is he trying to get enlightened? One last attempt at *satori*?

No! He is not chasing life, he is savouring his existence. He is basking in the moment-to-moment miracle of *being*. His nephew, on the other hand, is sleeping his life away. He is missing his life because he is chasing it, running after women, money, fame and status. Ryokan is *here*, *now*, while the nephew is lost.

Spirituality doesn't always have to be about dramatic experiences of enlightenment. It can direct our attention to something so ordinary that, at first glance, it doesn't seem that it could contain any wisdom at all.

We want to hear about enlightenment, not death and vulnerability. We already know about that. But the point is that we don't. We avoid death and vulnerability and become enthralled by abstract concepts like enlightenment, pure awareness and emptiness. We can chase these ideas as a way to avoid the waning of our lives but this will leave us completely unprepared.

It's by stopping and savouring our most basic functions, the daily processes that we take for granted: seeing, hearing, breathing, eating, walking, thinking and going to the bathroom, that we become grateful for the sheer intelligence and heart-breaking vulnerability that pours through our bodies and minds. At some point, all these functions begin to deteriorate.

The mind loves to chase big experiences. Our job is simply to recognise this wild goose chase and return to *this* experience, *this* moment, *this* life. The life that we did not ask for, the life that nevertheless, we have been granted.

We only stop when a friend dies, our child is sick, or we suddenly can't catch our next breath. The good news is that we don't have to wait to savour our own lives. We can do this now. This is why we practise, it's not to live in a perfect state of health or become a billionaire by asking the universe to make it so. We practise to know our own vulnerability, our own fragility, our own preciousness, again and again, and to remind others of their own vulnerability again and again.

Then we can understand what the 13th-century Christian mystic, Meister Eckhart, meant when he said that if there is only ever one prayer to leave our lips, it should be:

Thank You!

Take good care of yourself.

Epilogue: forget about it

I've travelled from Bristol to South London to attend a talk with a famous spiritual teacher. It's a summer day and I'm early so I stop off at a fashionable cafe for a cup of green tea and to scribble some thoughts in my notebook. The people at the table next to me enjoy a lazy brunch, debating the quickest way to get from Paris to Vienna, while outside a man carefully loads freshly baked baguettes into the panniers of his bicycle

I walk to the bathroom and as I open the door something familiar draws my eye. There is a tiny triskelion— the Celtic three-legged symbol of the Isle of Man— embossed into the antique brass door handle. A good omen, I think.

Thirty minutes later I've arrived at the huge community hall where the teacher will give his talk. Most of the chairs are already full and there is a group of raven- haired, olive-skinned young women wrapped in pashminas, huddled together on the floor in front of the stage. They remind me of groupies at a rock concert. I find a seat and wait.

Next to me a Frenchman named Kashi—the ancient name for Varanasi—weeps softly into his girlfriend's shoulder, whilst at the very back sits a dreadlocked Rastafarian—tall, noble and serene.

Finally, the spiritual teacher enters the room. He's dressed in white and wears strings of brown mala beads around his neck. Everyone's face lights up and they break into broad smiles as he moves through the crowd, embracing some people and playfully ruffling the hair of others. He has an aura of happiness, openness and fun.

He makes his way up to the front and sits on a chair carefully placed in the middle of the stage, next to a small collection of framed photographs of his own teachers. After a few minutes of silence he begins to talk, stopping now and again to ask the enraptured audience for questions. People raise their hands and are either handed a microphone or invited to come up onto the stage and sit next to him for a more intimate meeting.

I raise my hand several times, eager to ask the question which was burning me up inside like a red-hot coal, but others are chosen instead.

A woman is in tears because she feels she has lost the deep stillness she felt with him at their last meeting. The teacher asks her to close her eyes and then guides her back into herself, back into quietude, back into her own essence. She rests there, silent and serene whilst others ask about relationships, surrender and the nature of God.

And then, in no time at all it's over and the two hours seemed to have gone by in a flash. "One more question," he announces and again, I raise my hand. This time our eyes meet and he shouts, "Yes! You!" pointing me out. I feel like I've just won the lottery and waste no time in making my way through the crowd and stepping up onto the stage with him, microphone ready, the audience listening.

But as I begin to speak I realise that I've completely forgotten my question and so instead I just start describing my own experience of being nobody, and how I'm merged with each moment which has no centre or boundary and the sheer joy and relief and grace of that. The teacher is beaming at me. I run out of words and there's a moment of intense silence which fills the entire room. The silence which calls us all home.

Suddenly my mind bursts into action again and I remember the urgent question I had travelled here to ask and now had the unbelievable good fortune to do so.

"What is emptiness?" I ask.
"Ah, just forget about it!" He laughs.

Notes

Acknowledgements

I would never have imagined that such a short book would take so many years to write. Many of these chapters began life as spontaneous talks for my meditation group or as articles for my newsletter and it's taken many years to accumulate enough material together to create the book you are now holding, which—like everything else—is simply the consequence of an infinity of contributing factors. Just as the pages are created from trees and the ink made from pigment, each chapter has its roots in people and experiences, and without them this book would not exist.

I'm grateful to everyone who has in some way contributed to the finished version, but I would like to say thank you to the following people whose influences have been more prominent, whether they know it or not.

My parents, Michael and Fiona, for my life, my body, mind and personality. To my wife Sarah and our children, Leo and Primrose, for your continued support and for reminding me that being ordinary is the greatest joy. Tom Buckley Houston, my dharma brother and teacher, for years of deep conversations and for reminding me that I'm not Enlightened. Thank you to

Daniel Ruddock for reminding me that I am. Chris Arthur, for his inspiration years ago when I was an undergraduate at Lampeter University. The late Professor Nicholas Goodrick-Clarke for seeing my potential and introducing me to the wonders of the Western esoteric traditions. To my brother Adam Kendrick-Kewley, Leonie Gschwendtberger, Rob and Jo Smith, Matt and Jenny Kuhn-Shepherd, Richard Cox, Rod Orders, Steve Taylor and everyone else who gave me valuable feedback when this book was in its early stages. I'd also like to give special thanks to Piers Moore Ede for years of encouragement, often when I felt that I had nothing of importance to say.

I'd also like to thank all of my teachers, friends and students past, present and future, who continue to inspire and awaken me.

Thank you to Julian and Catherine at New Sarum Press for all their hard work and inspired editing. You have brought this book into existence.

I'd like to dedicate *The Treasure House* to the memory of my good friend Dave Payne (Bill) who passed away as I was finishing the book. His life was transformed by some of the insights and perspectives shared here, and his wise and accepting attitude to his terminal condition was itself a great teaching. Thank you, Bill. I'll see you in the trees, flowers and grass.

May we all be happy and well.

May we all awaken to the miracle of this moment

May we all realise our true nature.

CONVERSATIONS ON AWAKENING

Interviews by Iain and Renate McNay

Conversations on Awakening features 24 unique accounts of Awakening all taken from transcripts of interviews made for conscious.tv.

Some of the interviewees are renowned spiritual teachers while others are completely unknown having never spoken in public or written a book.

These conversations will hopefully encourage you, inspire you, and maybe even guide you to find out who you really are.

Conversations on Awakening: Part One features interviews with A.H Almaas, Jessica Britt, Sheikh Burhanuddin, Linda Clair, John Butler, Billy Doyle, Georgi Y. Johnson, Cynthia Bourgeault, Gabor Harsanyi, Tess Hughes, Philip Jacobs and Igor Kufayev.

Conversations on Awakening: Part Two features interviews with Susanne Marie, Debra Wilkinson, Richard Moss, Mukti, Miek Pot, Reggie Ray, Aloka (David Smith), Deborah Westmorland, Russel Williams, Jurgen Ziewe, Martyn Wilson and Jah Wobble.

Published by White Crow Books.
Available from Amazon in ebook and paperback format and to order from all good bookstores.

Part one: p.282, ISBN: 978-1786770936

Part two: p.286, ISBN: 978-1786770950

www.conscious.tv